CONCISE HANDBOOK
OF LINGUISTICS

CONCISE HANDBOOK
OF LINGUISTICS

A GLOSSARY OF TERMS

by
DANIEL J. STEIBLE, Ph.D.
Our Lady of Cincinnati College

PHILOSOPHICAL LIBRARY
New York

PREFACE

With the recent growth of interest in linguistics and a parallel growth in its terminology, the need for a glossary has become apparent. Courses in linguistics are being added to the curricula of more and more colleges and universities, and some aspects of the subject are finding their way into the secondary school and even to the elementary level in some places.

A glossary offers neither dictionary definitions nor information on an encyclopedic scale; this book, intended for the use of the student of English linguistics (the authority or expert needs no glossary), offers brief and, as far as possible, simplified explanations of terms in widespread use by linguists and teachers of linguistics, together with examples and, it is hoped, useful cross-references. Terms which are to be found in use more specifically among the "structuralists" or among the "transformationalists" are so noted. Since the student will very likely have been brought up in the environment of traditional or "school" grammar, some terms are explained in the light of the traditional in order to help him make the transition to the newer concepts. The student will come to know some terms from the textbook which he is using in class; others will be explained by his instructor, but when the student turns to supplementary reading, he will encounter terms that are new to him. It is this need which it is hoped this glossary will fill.

Some limitations, perhaps arbitrary, to the scope of this glossary have had to be established with the result that the following are not included herein: (1) almost all literary terms though frequently used by linguists, but with no special variation from their accepted meanings,

5

and all terms used in traditional grammar with the exception of a few which linguists use with some departure from the traditional meaning; (2) terms closely connected with the *history* of the English language, especially in its earlier stages; (3) terms connected with the organs of speech, a matter dealt with in an Appendix, although terms for the kinds of sounds, such as *labial* or *liquid*, are included; many of the more subtle details in the areas of phonetics and acoustics are excluded since most of this material is readily available in a number of sources;[1] (4) terms related to the use of the computer, sound spectrograph, stenosonograph, or other electronic devices for linguistic study, since any student who becomes involved with any such devices will, no doubt, be supplied with a special handbook on their use and operation.

There are a few terms so broad and capable of so many different interpretations that it would be impossible to deal with them within the scope of this compilation. One such term, for example, is "meaning."[2] In the index to one reference book on linguistics, there are no less than seventy references to various aspects of this term. However, the term is here included when qualified in some way, such as "lexical meaning" or "referential meaning." Some terms exist which have long been the subject of controversy, such as "morpheme." The student need not be concerned at first with the subtler points of difference as to the application of such terms, and so only a "working explanation" has been given.

A number of terms are so complicated that a full treatment would be out of place in a glossary; in such

1. An excellent beginning can be made with Ralph R. Leutenegger, *The Sounds of English,* Chicago, Scott, Foresman and Co., 1963.
2. Something of the scope of this term may be grasped from Charles Ogden and Ivor Richards, *The Meaning of Meaning,* New York, Harcourt, Brace and Co., 1936, and J. R. Firth, "Modes of Meaning," in *Essays and Studies,* Vol. 4, The English Association, 1951.

cases, a book or periodical article which will supply additional information is indicated.

As a matter of convenience to the student, an Appendix includes: (A) a list of symbols and abbreviations and their uses as commonly made by linguists; (B) a graphic representation of the physical apparatus which produces speech sounds; (C) a simplified but acceptable version of a phonemic alphabet; and (D) phonetic charts of the vowels, the consonants, and the vowel phonemes.

There are, no doubt, some terms which have been overlooked and hence are not listed in this glossary; indeed, there may be some explanations that are in error or faulty, at least in the view of some linguists. For this human weakness the compiler apologizes in advance since he can only attribute any such flaws, as Samuel Johnson once did, simply "to ignorance."

Daniel J. Steible

Our Lady of Cincinnati College
Cincinnati, Ohio

ACKNOWLEDGMENTS

Gratitude is expressed to the authors and publishers of the following books which have been, in one way or another, helpful in drawing up the explanations of linguistic terms which are here compiled.

Allen, Harold B. (Ed.): *Readings in Applied English Linguistics*, New York, Appleton-Century-Crofts, 1964.

Anderson, Wallace L. and Norman C. Stageberg (Eds.): *Introductory Readings on Language* (Rev. ed.), New York, Holt, Rinehart, and Winston, 1966.

Barber, Charles: *Linguistic Change in Present-Day English*, University, Alabama, The University of Alabama Press, 1964.

Bloomfield, Morton W. and Leonard Newmark: *A Linguistic Introduction to the History of English*, New York, Alfred A. Knopf, 1963.

Carroll, John B.: *The Study of Languages*, Cambridge, Mass., Harvard University Press, 1963.

Fodor, Jerry A. and Jerrol J. Katz: *The Structure of Language: Readings in the Philosophy of Language*, Englewood Cliffs, New Jersey, Prentice-Hall, Inc., 1964.

Francis, W. Nelson: *The Structure of American English*, New York, The Ronald Press Co., 1958.

       : *The English Language: An Introduction*, New York, W. W. Norton and Co., 1963.

Gleason, H. A. Jr.: *An Introduction to Descriptive Linguistics* (Rev. ed.), New York, Holt, Rinehart, and Winston, 1961.

Halliday, M. A. K., Angus McIntosh, and Peter Strevens: *The Linguistic Sciences and Language Teaching*, Bloomington, Indiana University Press, 1964.

Hill, Archibald A.: *Introduction to Linguistic Structures*, New York, Harcourt, Brace, and World, Inc., 1958.

Landar, Herbert: *Language and Culture*, New York, Oxford University Press, 1966.

Lehmann, Winifred P.: *Historical Linguistics: An Introduction*, New York, Holt, Rinehart, and Winston, 1962.

Leutenegger, Ralph R.: *The Sounds of American English: An Introduction to Phonetics*, Chicago, Scott, Foresman and Co., 1963.

Nist, John: *A Structural History of English*, New York, St. Martin's Press, 1966.

Quine, Willard V.: "The Problem of Meaning in Linguistics," in *From A Logical Point of View*, (2nd ed.), Cambridge, Mass., Harvard University Press, 1961.

Roberts, Paul: *Understanding Grammar*, New York, Harper and Bros., 1954.

Robins, R. H.: *General Linguistics, An Introductory Survey*, Bloomington, The University of Indiana Press, 1964.

Thomas, Owen: *Transformational Grammar and the Teaching of English*, New York, Holt, Rinehart, and Winston, 1965.

Waterman, John T.: *Perspective in Linguistics*, Chicago, The University of Chicago Press, 1963.

accidence

the term refers to the study of grammatical inflections, a phase of the broader area of syntax.

accidental assimilation

a phonemic change or assimilation (q.v.) which comes about by accident as when a certain pronunciation proves too difficult for some speakers' organs of articulation, as in the pronunciation of *length* as if it rhymed with *tenth*.

acronym

a word formed by combining the initial letters or syllables of a series of related words, as *NATO, radar, Alcoa*.

acrophony

the alphabetic principle that there is a grapheme (q.v.) in the writing system for each phoneme in the phonological system.

action nominal

a nominal (q.v.) formed by a verb plus the {-ing} ending; it resembles the traditional gerund, as in
    Living in the country can be fun.
    John was interrupted by the *ringing* of the door-bell.

acuteness

an acoustic characteristic of the English language whereby there is a sharp articulation of the front vowels / i e æ / and the apical and post-apical consonants.

addition

a term in generative grammar denoting a transformation

rule symbolized as a → a + b, as in the derivation *She couldn't go* from *She could go.*

additive morpheme

a morpheme so classified by its use when added to one or more other morphemes; the additive morphemes are stems, prefixes, infixes, and suffixes.

adjectival

a word of adjective function formed from a noun, as *bearded* from *beard, American* from *America, comfortable* from *comfort, etc.*

adjectivalization morpheme

a morpheme which, added to a noun or a verb, produces an adjective form; among the more common are:
{-able} *peace, peaceable;* {-ate} *passion, passionate;* {-ful} *shame, shameful;* {-ish} *book, bookish;* {-y} *wind, windy;* {-ant} *defy, defiant;* {-ing} *dote, doting.*

adjectiveform

the form of a word in which it functions as a determiner, usually recognized as having a distinguishing position in a structure.

adjunct

in structural grammar, a noun acting as modifier and standing in the position immediately preceding the head (q.v.), thus coming between the adjective(s) and the head; also a prepositional phrase or an adverb, characteristically set off by a juncture or by junctures and capable of filling any of four positions in a sentence of normal construction; note how the adjunct *frequently* may be moved about in the sentence — *The president calls meetings frequently.*

adjunctival

a fixed phrase with an adverbial function, such as *meanwhile, hereafter, afterward, just now*, etc.

adverbform

the form of a word in which it functions as modifier of a determiner and is identified by its position in a structure.

adverbial morpheme

the morpheme {-ly} which, added to certain adjectives, produces the adverbial form, as *quick, quickly*.

affix

a bound syllabic morpheme attached to a base or root (q.v.) as a prefix (*pre*dict), a suffix (dic*tion*), or an infix (re*in*duction).

affricate

a stop (q.v.) which is released gradually rather than abruptly, causing a slight friction noise; also called affricated stop.

agentive nominal

a transformed verb form which produces a name for the agent who performs a particular action, as
    Mary is a *writer* of verse.
    Rex is an excellent *actor*.

agglutinating analog

a fixed form arrived at by use of the principle of analogy, the process involving the addition of affixes or suffixes.

13

agglutination

a process of word formation in which the morphemes, as constituent meaningful elements, retain their characteristic forms rather than blend with surrounding elements, as in *wishbone, frogman, bedroom.*

agreement morpheme

the same as tense morpheme (q.v.).

allograph

a variant spelling for the same sound; for example, in Old English *ea* and *ae* were sounded alike; the modern *w* developed, as its name indicates, from *uu.*

allologs

different forms of a word which differ only in their inflectional affixes, as *hope, hoped, hoping, hopeful, hopes.*

allomorphs

a term applied to a sub-class of morphemes which consists of like morphs (q.v.) that are in complementary distribution with all other members of their morpheme; for example, {s}, {-es}, {-en}, and {ø} are allomorphs of the plural morpheme, the zero allomorph {ø} accounting for cases where the plural is the same as the singular.

allophones

the different sounds that may represent a phoneme (q.v.) in the speech of a given speaker, that is, phonetically similar sounds which do not interfere with each other.

allophrase

a variant of a phrase, not influencing meaning in any significant manner, as *It is warm* and *It's warm* or *He cannot go* and *He can't go.*

alternants

the different (usually two) pronunciations which may exist for the same word, as *house* in *He purchased the house* and *Where shall we house the new students?* Such words are said to have multiple allomorphs. To put it another way, an alternant is a phoneme which may alternate with another phoneme according to accompanying phonemes.

alveolar

the hard ridge behind the upper front teeth; an alveolar consonant, such as *s* or *z*, is produced when the tongue touches or nears this ridge.

alveopalatal

the consonant sounds produced when the blade and front of the tongue touch or approach the alveolar ridge and the hard palate; the consonants are / c j s z / .

ambisyllabic position

the position of a single consonant phoneme between vowels, called ambisyllabic because it belongs partly to each of the syllables on either side; for example, {t̪}, {t̬}, and {r̥}, which occur between vowels, are classed by some linguists as allophones of both / t / and / d / .

amelioration

a semantic shift in which, during the historical evolution of a language, the meaning of a word is improved or bettered in some way, as the word *sturdy* which once meant "harsh and rough" came to mean "hardy and vigorous."

amphiboly

the ambiguity in meaning of an entire sentence though no word in the sentence is itself ambiguous, as in "I shall lose no time in answering your letter."

analogic change

a change in some aspect of language — a verb form, for example — based on the principle of analogy by which things are made alike because it seems that they ought to be alike, such as the change from a "strong" verb to a "weak" verb.

analytic syntax

the syntax (q.v.) of a language in which word order determines grammatical function.

anomalous verb

one of that class of verbs which form their present and past tenses from different roots; sometimes referred to as "strong verbs;" the common examples in English are *am, was* and *go, went*.

anthropological linguist

a student of language, especially as it relates to the origin, development, beliefs, customs, and the like, of a people or of peoples.

antithetical polyseme

term indicates the assumption that a word, because of a historical shift of sense, may come to mean the opposite of its earlier or original meaning.

apical

a term used to describe those consonants articulated with the tip of the tongue, such as *d* or *t*.

appositive

a noun or nominal structure which modifies a noun head which it immediately follows; it is usually marked by single-bar junctures before and after, as
My son / the chemical engineer / gave a talk.

arch

the name for the symbol ⌢ sometimes used for concatenation (q.v.).

area linguistics

the study of language on a geographical basis; dialectology (q.v.).

articulation

in general, the movement of the organs of speech in producing a speech sound; also may refer to the speech sound itself, especially a consonant.

articulators

the movable organs of speech which can modulate tone or produce secondary sounds; they include the lips, tongue, velum, uvula, upper teeth, alveolar ridge, and palate. See Appendix B.

articulatory phonetics

the term for that branch of phonetics (q.v.) which studies the production of speech sounds by the human vocal tract.

aspect

as a technical linguistic term, refers to the timespan or completedness of an action as indicated by a verb form; in English, the most common aspects are: beginning (He *started* to walk away); continuing (He *kept* on blowing the horn); and completed (He *ended* his speech abruptly). Note that this word is used in its more general sense of *phase* or *part* at many points elsewhere in this book; also, any phase (q.v.) or fraction of a phase of a given segment that is coterminous (limited by the same boundaries) with that segment.

aspirated stop

the result when an articulator releases the breath abruptly with an audible "puff" before the next sound begins.

assimilation

the process by which one sound is changed to a second sound because of the influence of a third; for example, the negative prefix *-in* has the allomorph *-im* which appears before /p/ and /b/, as in *impertinent* and *imbalance*.

attribute

the same as modifier (q.v.).

automatic alternation

when a formal alternation of phonemes is regularly determined by the phonemes of accompanying forms, the alternation is said to be automatic, as the alternation of [-s], [-z], or [-ez] in the English plural is determined by the final phoneme of the noun stem. (For details, see Rulon S. Wells, "Automatic Alternation," in *Language*, Vol. 25, Linguistic Society of America, 1949.)

auxiliary verb

a form of a class of verbs which, combined with a main
verb, produces all the tenses except the present and the
past; such verbs fall into three types: the modal (q.v.),
to have, and *to be.*

back-formation

the creation by analogy of a new word from an existing word, through a mistaken notion that the existing word is a derivative of the new word, as *enthuse* from *enthusiasm*.

back vowels

a group of five vowels, all rounded: [u], [ʊ], [o], [ɔ], and [ɒ]. See Appendix D.

barred I

the name given to the vowel phoneme represented by / ɨ / , a variant of the sound / i / .

base

the morpheme in a word which carries the principal part of the meaning of the whole. See stem and root.

base adjective

a regular adjective which contains no derivational suffix, that is, has not been converted into an adjective from some other category, such as *good, large, hot, pretty, happy, quick;* the comparative and superlative are formed by adding the suffixes {-er} and {-est}; the noun form is produced by adding the suffix {-ness}, and the adverb form by adding {-ly}, as in *quick, quicker, quickest, quickness, quickly*.

base morpheme

the root or base to which prefixes, suffixes, or infixes are attached in forming derivatives (q.v.) as *boy* in *boyish* or *-duce* in *reduce*.

bilabial stop

the sounds of the consonants / p / and / b / produced by forcing air through the closed lips just as they open to release.

binary

a tendency of the language to display a "two-part" quality in its grammatical constructions.

binary analysis

a method of linguistic description whereby a structure is seen as consisting of two parts, such as noun phrase (or cluster) and verb phrase (or cluster), each of which may be further subdivided until all parts in a given structure are accounted for.

binary cut

the division of a construction into two parts when making an immediate constituent (q.v.) analysis.

binits

the units of measurement of information (q.v.); for example, a "code" with two alternative signals which are equally likely to be used has a capacity of one binit per use; in practice, it is not as simple as this since frequency of use and repetition must be considered. (For a detailed treatment, see H. A. Gleason, *An Introduction to Descriptive Linguistics* (Rev. ed.), New York, Holt, Rinehart, and Winston, 1961, Chap. 23.)

blade spirant

the s-like sounds produced by channeling the blade of the tongue so as to project a jet of air; also called sibilant.

blend

a word of non-humorous usage created by telescoping parts of two distinct words, such as *astronaut, phonovision, paratroop.*

blending

making a new word by putting together parts of existing words in a new combination; the humorous variety is usually called a portmanteau word (q.v.), but there are others which are given serious usage, such as *linotype* and *bureaucrat.*

bound allomorph

an allomorph which appears only with a particular morpheme, as in the case of the terminal allomorph of *house* used as a verb / *hawz* /.

bound base

any base (or stem) which must always be combined with one or more other morphemes, as in the case of {*-turb*} or {*cred-*}.

bound morpheme

a morpheme which does not occur alone, but is attached to one or more other morphemes, one of which will be a base; all affixes and declensional endings are bound morphemes, as in *ad*-vance, *con*-spire, king-*dom*, deliver-*ance*.

branching tree diagram

the method devised by transformationalist grammarians to present graphically the structure of a sentence and to diagram transformations.

breath-group

a span of the stream of speech (of words uttered) limited

by one exhalation of breath; the spans are separated from each other by rather rapid inhalations.

bundle of isoglosses

the result when a number of isoglosses (q.v.) move across a dialect area and pile up at or near the boundary.

C

calque

the same as loan-translation (q.v.).

case-form

the form of a word (noun) as determined by the case which it represents, that is, one of the seven cases in a declension.

categories

classifications of words in English by functional meanings determined by position, and by class-meanings determined by form-classes (q.v.) composed of all forms having the same function; categories in English include object, number, actor, action, goal, numbered object, and predicative action.

catenative verb

a group or chain of words which function together as a verb, as *seemed to believe*, or *used to suppose*.

central vowels

a group of seven vowels, two of which, [ə], and [ɨ], usually occur in unstressed syllables; one, [ɒ], is found chiefly in diphthongs; and four, [ɜ], [e], [ʌ], [a], occur as syllabic vowels in stressed syllables. See Appendix D.

citation form

the manner in which a phonemic structure is written when it is used as a linguistic illustration; the form is enclosed in square brackets [ ].

class-changing derivation

the addition of an affix which produces a derived form

of another class, as *kind* is an adjective, add suffix -ly to produce *kindly*, an adverb; or *prison*, a noun, add prefix *im-* to produce *imprison*, a verb.

class-maintaining derivation

the addition of an affix which does not cause the word to undergo a change of class, as *child* is a noun, add suffix *-hood* to produce *childhood*, also a noun; or *king*, a noun, add suffix *-dom* to produce *kingdom*, also a noun.

clicks

sounds produced by closing the oral passage, drawing the tongue downward with a sudden release; these sounds are not phonemically significant in English.

clipping

the morphological shortening of polysyllabic words, an abbreviation of a sort, as *auto* from *automobile* or *ad* from *advertisement*.

clitic

an unaccented word, having lost its accent by appearing in a phrase but with phrase stress; it is proclitic if it lacks stress when it appears before another word in the same phrase; it is enclitic when it appears after another word in the same phrase.

close juncture

three forms of juncture (q.v.) are called close because they momentarily close off the flow of speech; these three forms of suprasegmental phonemes (q.v.) of transition define word-group boundaries. See Symbols $/ \mid /$, $/ \mid\mid /$, $/ \# /$.

closed classes

classes made up of function words (q.v.) whose membership is more stable than other classes and less likely to change.

closure

the result when the oral cavity is completely closed by placing the tongue against the roof of the mouth or by pressing the lips firmly together; in addition, the velum will prevent air from passing through the nose; the sound involved is called a stop.

coda

according to one way of classifying phonemes, that part of a phonemic syllable which follows the peak (q.v.).

cognate

a word allied to another word by derivation from the same source or root, as English *apple* and German *apfel,* or English *mother* and Latin *mater.*

collocation

an arrangement of words established by usage, usually that of a given time or historical period; in lexicography, the term is applied to word combinations which help to clarify the meanings of the words involved.

colloquialism

a word or structure used in the conversation of cultivated people and in informal writing, such as personal letters, as distinguished from formal writing; not to be confused with localism (q.v.); most linguists hold that no stigma attaches to the use of colloquialisms.

color

the distinguishing auditory effect of a vowel which is always able to be perceived regardless of the length of the vowel in its position in the center or nucleus of a syllable.

colorless l

the high-central vowel /ɨ/, lacking any perceptible distinguishing auditory effect, as in the second syllable of *women* /wimɨn/ or in *regimen* /regimɨn/.

compactness

a distinctive acoustic feature of English produced by a central formant region, such as characterizes the articulation of the low vowels / æ a ɔ / and the back consonants / h k g ŋ w /.

comparative linguistics

the study of language chiefly concerned with the comparison of linguistic forms at different points in the historical development of a language; also the study of the interrelationships of languages, classifying them into families, such as Germanic, Semitic, Romance.

comparative morpheme

the morpheme {-er} which, added to the adjective, produces the comparative degree, as *quick, quicker.*

comparative reconstruction

in historical linguistics, the study and comparison of the oldest surviving records of the various languages which make up a language family, such as the Indo-European family.

complement

a constituent whose function is to fill out or complete the meaning of another constituent in the same construction.

complementary distribution

the term refers to the fact that phones (q.v.) which usually appear in a particular environment cannot appear in each other's places, that is, one phone is distinguished from another by reason of their separate environments.

complex

a term used to classify sentences in which one predication is a subordinate element.

complex vowel

a term applied to the result when a simple vowel appears in an environment where it occurs with one of the three semivowel offset glides /y w h/; in theory, the complex vowels (traditionally diphthongs) are twenty-seven in number.

composite verb

in transformational grammar, a verb of two constituent parts used in a structure in which the object stands between the two parts of the verb, as in *sent* her *away*, or *caught* him *cheating*; the verb itself, *sent away*, consists of a verb stem and complement.

composition

the formation of a new word by the joining together of two existing words into a compound, such as *hotbed* or *whitewash*.

compound

a term used to classify sentences containing more than one predication.

compound word

a word formed by the union of two or more free morphemes, with the stress pattern usually falling from maximum /´/ to minor /ˋ/, as in *ráilròad* or *bóxing boùt*.

concatenation

the process of stringing together a set of linguistic elements.

concatenation of strings

in generative grammar, this term denotes the entire range of grammatical representations of the permitted sentences in a language.

concord

grammatical agreement of related parts of speech, as the plural form of a verb in concord with the plural form of a noun.

concretization

a category of semantic change whereby a word naming an abstract quality becomes the basis for the means of making the abstraction tangible and visible, as *youngness* becomes *young man*, while *kindness* and *mercy* have been concretized into the plural forms, *kindnesses* and *mercies*.

consonantality

a distinctive acoustic feature of English that forms non-syllabic phonemic nuclei.

constituent

any one of the smaller structural units linked together in a construction (q.v.).

constituent analysis

a term related to binary analysis (q.v.), the method based on the concept that English sentences consist of a series of levels on each of which there are two parts.

constituent sentence

in transformational grammar, an embedded sentence, traditionally called a dependent clause.

constituent structure

in transformational grammar, any string of comparatively simple structures which may become a phrase structure in a transformation; also a level of grammatical relationship such as exists between questions and declaratives by reason of the presence of a functional *wh*, as illustrated by *Someone will visit her* transformed to *Will someone visit her?* which is symbolized as S→ (wh) Nominal-Predicate.

constriction

the result when the oral cavity is narrowed by the action of the tongue, lips, and velum, producing friction; the sound which results is a spirant (q.v.).

construct (as a noun)

the term refers to instances where one of a group of uninflectible words, which may be either prepositions or adverbs, is combined with another word to create a semantic unit, such as *setup* or *upstairs*; not to be confused with constructional (q.v.).

construction

a grammatical unit made up of smaller units linked by a grammatical connection, as a sentence is made up of a noun phrase and a verb phrase, as in —
   S→ NP + VP.

constructional

the term for a structure in which an uninflectible word (adverb or preposition) appears with a verb but not joined to the verb base, and is identifiable as an adverbial, as in *sent up*, *up* is an adverbial; not to be confused with construct (q.v.).

context

the term refers to the words in the environment of a given word and to the grammatical structure of which it is a part; the means by which the intended meaning of a word in a given instance is selected from among its several meanings.

context-free grammar

a phrase-structure grammar in which the *a* of a rule $a \rightarrow b$ must be a single symbol and may not include the context in which the change is to be brought about.

context-sensitive grammar

a phrase-structure type of grammar in which the symbols of the rules include the necessary context in which a change is to be brought about.

context sensitivity

the process of selection and adjustment which goes on in the mind of a reader or listener as he interprets those meanings of words which best fit with each other, a kind of circle of contextual influence; in generative grammar, context sensitivity is said to be essential in determining only and all the sentences of English.

contextual meanings

the different meanings or shades of meaning which a word may convey under the influence of different contexts or environments.

continuance

an acoustic feature of English that does not impede the

flow of speech breath, as in all vowels, semivowels, and certain consonants.

contoid

a term applied to any non-vocoid. See vocoid.

contrastive distribution

the term refers to contrasts in sound, especially when the difference in sound is sufficient to produce different words, as /k/ and /t/ contrast, illustrated by *skiff* and *stiff*; not to be confused with complementary distribution (q.v.).

convergence

the drawing together of two (or more) words during the course of language development to the point where they have a common morpheme and usually some relationship in meaning, as *scribe* and *script*, or *bell* and *belfry*.

conversion

the transfer of a word from one word-class to another, as *to screen* (to verb from noun), *to service* (to verb from noun), and *hair-do* (to noun from the verb phrase *do the hair*).

co-occurrence

the dependence of one morpheme on the occurrence of some other morpheme in the same sentence or close by so that a change in one is reflected by a change in the other; this is illustrated by two statements or by a question and answer in discourse wherein certain elements in the second statement or in the answer are present because of certain ones in the first statement or in the question, as in "This is *361-2401*; what *number* did you want?" "Oh, I must have *dialed* the wrong *number*."

coordinator

one of a group of function words or phrases, representing one way of joining two or more syntactically equivalent units to form a structure of coordination (q.v.) which then functions as a single unit; some examples are *and, but, not, along with, neither . . . nor.*

copulative verb

also called linking verb, a structural link between a subject and a complement; the more common copulatives include parts of the verb *to be*, verbs of the senses, verbs of appearance, and a few special cases.

core group

a term used to specify a sub-group within one of the larger classes, such as the adjectives or the adverbs, for purposes of some special classification.

corpus

a collection of sample utterances which have been gathered by a linguist for the purpose of analysis.

correct

representing acceptable usage, more specifically, a linguist would say that *I done it* is correct in relation to the dialect in which this usage occurs.

countable set

in set theory, the smallest kind of infinite set which can be put into one-to-one correspondence with the set of all possible integers; also called denumerable set.

count noun

in transformational grammar, a noun similar to the traditional concrete noun, to be distinguished from the mass/ abstract noun (q.v.); a count noun can always be preceded by a cardinal number, as *two girls, three ships, one dog.*

covert gender

the attribution of gender to animate or inanimate objects, without regard to sex, as a matter of rhetorical license, as in using *she* for a ship, sometimes for the moon, *etc.*

cultural context

all of the cultural aspects of a community or society in which language operates at a given time, and by which language may be influenced.

cultural levels

the cultural strata in a community established according to the degree to which the culture of the community has been absorbed by the individual; such levels in terms of language are variously described by such terms as "local dialect," "ungrammatical," "excessive use of slang," and others.

cut

that point in a structure (commonly a sequence of morphemes) at which a plus or open juncture occurs.

D

dead metaphor

a metaphor that has become so much a part of everyday usage that no one thinks of it as a metaphor, such as *an engine "knocks," prices are "cut" or "slashed," the "hands" of the clock.*

deep structure

the term refers to the observation by linguists that two sentences which seem quite similar display more subtle meanings and implications, as illustrated by such instances as:

She hoped Mary would go to the game with Jack.

She persuaded Mary to go to the game with Jack..

Something of the sense of deep structure is shown if both sentences are re-written in the passive voice:

She hoped Mary would be taken to the game by Jack.

She persuaded Mary to be taken to the game by Jack.

Notice in each pair who needs to be persuaded.

degree adverbial

a word of adverbial function which is indicative of degree, as *very* young, *quite* pretty, *rather* late; a number of adjectives may be transformed into degree adverbials, as *extreme-ly, thorough-ly.*

deictic

having a demonstrative or pointing function, as the pronouns *this* (near at hand) and *that* (some distance away).

deletion

in generative grammar, this is a transformation rule symbolized as $a + b \rightarrow b$, as in the derivation of *Mary rode* from *Mary rode the bicycle.*

dental sound

the sound represented by /θ/ and /ð/, produced by momentarily touching the tip of the tongue to the upper teeth.

denumerable set

same as countable set (q.v.).

derivation

the process of producing a sentence in transformational grammar; also the process by which words are fitted to different categories by adding suffixes to a basic stem, as sharp (adjective), sharp*ness* (noun), sharp*en* (verb), and sharp*ly* (adverb).

derivational contrast

a type of derivational change in lexical words by the addition or deletion of a suffix, as *curious* becomes *curiously* or *idly* becomes *idle*.

derivational suffix

a noun-marking suffix which may be added to bases or other words usually belonging to other parts of speech; some typical examples of such suffixes:
added to verbs, {-*age*} in *breakage*
{-*ance*} in *contrivance*
added to adjectives, {-*ity*} in *facility*
{-*ness*} in *coldness*
added to other nouns, {-*ian*} in *librarian*
{-*ster*} in *gangster*
added to a base, {-*er*} in *porter*
{-*ism*} in *theism*.

derivative

a word developed from another by the addition of one or more bound morphemes.

derived adjective

the term refers to adjectives formed from bound stems or bases by means of one of a group of derivational suffixes, such as {-ous} and {-able}, in *ominous* and *palatable;* they often form phrasal comparatives and superlatives through the use of the qualifiers *more* and *most;* transformed frequently from nouns or verbs, such adjectives usually describe accidental attributes, as in *dancing* teacher, *baked* beans, *childish* prattle, *joyful* occasion.

descriptive linguistics

that branch of linguistic study which is concerned with description of a language in terms of its own characteristic structure; scholars in this area are seeking a general theory of language structure within the framework of which they may understand the language under study.

deterioration

the same as pejoration (q.v.).

determinant

in a compound made by the combination of two or more words, the non-dominant or differentiating part, as in *rainbow*, which is essentially a *bow*, but *rain* differentiates this bow from other possible kinds; the determinant is the cooperating factor in a compound with the determinatum (q.v.).

determinative

a variation of determiner (q.v.) but especially applied to a noun with a case suffix modifying another noun, as in "This is *Smith's* house;" the term is also applied to the suffix which forms the determinative.

determinatum

in a compound made by the combination of two or more

words, the grammatically dominant part which undergoes inflection, is called the determinatum, as in *hayloft*,
haylofts; in some compound words, neither part actually
serves as determinatum by being grammatically dominant,
and one must simply know from usage what the word
means, as *hunchback* or *run-around*.

determiner

a constituent which modifies a head (q.v.), not to be confused with qualifier (q.v.) which modifies other kinds of
constituents.

diachronic linguistics

the study of a language or a linguistic feature through the
course of its historical evolution or development; distinct
from synchronic (q.v.).

diacritical marks

also called diacritics, the symbols or signs used to indicate
subtle phonetic variations; in English there are eight such
marks; syllabic [ˌ]; voiceless [ₒ]; voiced [ᵥ]; aspirated
[ᶜ]; rounded [ᵤ]; unrounded [ₘ]; fortis [ₙ]; and lenis [ᵤ],
there are also two shift signs: forward [ˌ], and backward [.].

diacritic grapheme

a grapheme that has no phonemic reference of its own
but has an influence upon the phonemic reference of a
neighboring grapheme (q.v.); the grapheme <e> is the
most versatile in English; for example, it can cause the
lengthening of a preceding single consonant, as in *hate*, it
indicates the /s/ value of <c>, as in *choice*; other graphemes which serve in this manner include <i>, <h>,
and <t>.

dialect

a version of a language distinguished by its peculiar idiom, vocabulary, phonology, and morphology; a given dialect is customarily associated with a specific geographic area.

dialectology

the branch of linguistic study concerned with dialects (q.v.).

diaphonemes

slight variations in sound which are in contrast to the over-all pattern of a language or to a dialect pattern.

differential meaning

traceable to Bloomfield, this term refers, not to a specific semantic meaning of a semantic type, but rather to the meaning of a form as being the same as or different from that of another form; used as a tool by structural linguistics.

diffuseness

a distinctive acoustic feature of English, produced by the absence of a central formant region, which characterizes the high vowels / i ɨ u / and the apical and post-apical consonants / s š z ž t c d j θ ä n l r /.

diffusion

the spread of linguistic elements by reciprocal borrowing of words by speakers of different languages which are, however, members of a language family.

digraph

a pair of letters which, taken together, represent a single phoneme, such as the (ge) in *manageable* represents / j /; also refers to a pair of graphemes each of which may have independent use in other circumstances, but in this instance used as a single grapheme, as in commonplace {th} and {qu}.

diphthong

syllabics which show a marked glide from one vowel position to another, as in *noise* / *oy* /, *loud* / *aw* /; also the blend of two consonantal phones into one phonemic unit, as *shy* / *s* /, *chain* / *c* /.

diplonomy

meaning literally, rule by two laws, the term denotes the dual control exercised over language on the one hand by physiological and acoustic factors, on the other simultaneously by linguistic factors; in a sense, the two factors may "conflict" and produce an ungrammatical expression, such as *these boy*. (For further discussion, see Martin Joos, "Semology: A Linguistic Theory of Meaning," in *Studies in Linguistics*, Vol. 13, Nos. 3, 4, 1958.)

directive function

the use of language for the purpose of causing or preventing overt action, that is, language formed into commands and requests; distinct from expressive function (q.v.).

discontinuous constituent

the term refers to the splitting of the predicate into two parts when a statement is transformed into a question by inverting the subject with the first auxiliary of the verb phrase in the predicate, as in You *are going* home, *Are* you *going* home?

disjunction

a succession of two or more segments (q.v.), interrupted by one segment or dyad (q.v.).

disjuncture

a postulated phoneme which represents the separation

between phonemic word-groups and is symbolized by a space, as /cde fghi/, though some linguists use the juncture /+/.

displaced speech

a term indicative of man's ability to speak of absent or abstract things as if they were physically present and concrete.

distinctive acoustic features

the basic phonemic oppositions within a language; in English there are seven: vocality / consonantality, tension / laxness, interruption / continuance, gravity / acuteness, compactness / diffuseness, nasality / orality, and stridency / mellowness.

distinguishers

the terms assigned to a lexical unit which are intended to reflect what is idiosyncratic about the meaning of that item; distinguishers attach to final meanings of a lexical unit, terminal to the lines developed by the semantic markers (q.v.).

distribution

in general, a term indicating the entire area covered by a phone-type, or class of minimal segments of speech, or all the kinds of environment in which it can occur; synonymous with range (q.v.); also refers to the number of different ways in which a word element may be used as a member of different form-classes, each of which is made up of all words that can appear in the same position in a given construction; the distribution of an element constitutes its environment.

distributional environment

the group of phones in a structure which appear with

a particular phone whose position cannot be filled by a different phone; see complementary distribution.

divergence

the drawing apart of two (or more) words during the course of language development to the point where they cease to contain the same morpheme, despite a relationship in meaning, as *plaintiff* and *plaintive*, or *sniff* and *snuff*.

dorsal sound

a sound produced by placing the back of the tongue against the soft palate, as in [k] and [g].

double bar juncture

the juncture, or transition from one linguistic structure to the next, which is marked by the rising intonation which follows a statement expressed as a question, such as *You're there?* or the question without a question word, such as *Is she coming?* See Symbols in Appendix A.

double cross juncture

the type of transition from one language element to the next which is marked by voice fade-out and usually by a lowering of pitch, and which appears at the end of structures at the point where periods are used, as well as at the end of questions which begin with question words, such as *What are you doing?* and *When is she coming?*

downgrading

the reduction in status of a language element, such as, for example, from the status of an independent sentence to that of a sentence element within a larger structure, as *The girl dyed her hair* is downgraded in *The girl who dyed her hair won the prize*; similar downgrading may occur in the case of various other sentence elements.

downturn

a term designating a drop or lowering in pitch such as occurs at the end of a declarative structure, particularly the sentence, accompanied by the double-cross juncture /#/ which corresponds to a period, sometimes to a semi-colon.

durative aspect

that form of a verb composed of the auxiliary *be* and the present participle, as in *is speaking, am coming.*

dyad

a sequence (q.v.) of only two segments (q.v.), thus a sub-class of sequences.

elliptical structure

a structure of coordination (q.v.) in which a single component is assumed to be functioning in two different positions, as in *I ordered plain peanuts, not salted,* the word *peanuts* (*or ones*) is understood following the word *salted.*

embedded adjective

an adjective enclosed within a constituent structure in a matrix sentence (q.v.), as in "He was voted the student who is *most likely* to succeed," which can be transformed into "He was voted the student *most likely* to succeed."

emotional symbolism

that aspect of language whereby linguistic elements are seen as symbols which in particular times and places take on special emotional significance or exercise a specific emotional appeal; this may extend from the words themselves to the way in which they are pronounced; examples may be found in most political speeches prior to an election.

emphatic (or affirmative) morpheme

the morpheme in a structure which is given emphasis by means of maximum stress and a rising inflection (as by use of italics when written), as in "I *have* closed the door."

empty word

a word that has no lexical content in itself, but does have grammatical function, such as the preposition *at,* the indefinite article *a,* or the auxiliary verb *could.*

encliticize

the speech characteristic of pronouncing a word as part of

the preceding word with accompanying loss of independent
accent, as to encliticize *not* in the sentence, *Mary isn't*
coming.

endocentric

indicates a construction having a head (q.v.) and one or
more modifiers (q.v.).

equivalent environments

in cases where two elements occur in environments which
are almost but not quite identical, these elements may be
said to be equivalent because they occur in the same
environment, as *The robins nest in the spring. The tulips*
bloom in early April; thus *The robins nest* and *The tulips*
bloom occur in equivalent environments.

etymology

the history of a word as demonstrated by analysis of its
basic parts or by indicating its origin and its evolutionary
development in form and meaning.

etymon

the form from which another form has developed, usually
with reference to the earliest form known.

exocentric

the term refers to a construction in which no constituent
serves as a head (q.v.), since there is none present which
can substitute for the entire construction, as *the clown*
laughed.

expansion

in generative grammar, a transformation rule symbolized
as $a \rightarrow b + c$, as in the derivation of *I helped Mary pack*
her books from *I helped Mary.*

expressive alternants

morphemes which function on the level of stimulus-response rather than on a semantic level, and which are usually determined by other morphemes within the same word, as exemplified by *allergic* and *allergy*, or *lionize* and *leonine*.

expressive function

the use of language for the purpose of communicating feelings or emotions rather than to cause or prevent action or to impart factual information. See directive function.

expressive meaning

the relation of a sign (or symbol) considered as a stimulus to the response which it elicits or expresses.

expressivism

that aspect or characteristic of language concerned with the behavioral meanings of words as stimuli to response which may influence the design of a word at different stages of its growth; this aspect is of special interest to etymologists and psycholinguists.

extension

a category of semantic change in which the meaning of a word is broadened from a narrow application to a more general one, as the word *ticket* once referred only to a slip of paper which admitted one to the theatre, but has since been extended to the permit to ride on some form of public transportation or to attend a wide variety of social or athletic affairs.

external reconstruction

the use of comparisons with relatable languages in order

to support inference about an earlier stage in a language.

extrapolation

the projection of what is not yet known on the basis of data that have already been determined.

F

factitive suffix

a suffix which conveys the meaning of "make," as {-ize} in *legal-ize,* to make legal; *tranquil-ize,* to make tranquil.

factive nominal

the term refers to the combination of *that* followed by a sentence structure, the combination serving as subject or object of a certain kind of sentence, such as *That* he is learned is true, or Mary hoped *that* Jack would call her.

falling terminal juncture

another name for double-cross juncture (q.v.).

fascicle of isoglosses

the same as bundle of isoglosses (q.v.).

feature

grammatical feature, a simple fact of grammatical arrangement, as *doc* precedes *tor.*

finite sequence

an ordered series of consecutive linguistic units, such as phonemes, taken as a sample of a supposedly infinite variety of such sequences.

fixed phrase

a type of predeterminer (q.v.) regarded as a stereotyped expression, such as *lots of, a couple of;* also a group of words forming an entity which functions as a unit and which has a stress construction markedly different from that which is characteristic of a corresponding free phrase; as illustration, note the contrast in stress pattern between *the grêen hóuse*, which is free, and *the gréenhoùse*, which is fixed.

flap

a sound made by touching some part of the tongue very briefly to another point of articulation and bringing it away abruptly before the quality of a stop or affricate can be heard.

flexion

a characteristic of a language which makes it possible to list new expressions of action under one heading; if a new word were coined which ended in {-ize}, it would most likely be recognized as a verb, not a noun.

focal area

in the study of dialect, the apparent major cultural center of a dialect area as shown when the isoglosses are bunched somewhat closely together and at quite even distance from such a center.

forestress

applicable to the stress given a compound word when maximum stress is placed upon the first syllable, as in *shówroòm* or *páydày*.

form

in a general sense, a kind or type; more specifically, a given word considered under some aspect of function or syntax; in a still more technical linguistic sense, one of the bases upon which classification and analysis of a language may be built, and in this sense it is concerned with such elements as parts of speech, word relationships, inflectional endings, and the like. (For more details see W. Nelson Francis, "Revolution in Grammar," in *Quarterly Journal of Speech*, Vol. 40, Speech Association of America, 1954.)

form class

that group or collection of words which can appear in the same position in a given construction, such as simple verbs, regular adjectives, singular nouns; some words can belong to more than one form class according to usage, as *"building* a house," "enter the *building."*

formative (as a noun)

the term is applied to a morpheme which is bound in the sense that it never appears alone, but not bound in the sense of being rigidly restricted as to its environment, as the suffix {-*dom*} in *kingdom, wisdom.*

form word

in transformational grammar, one of a certain class of words which provides the substance of a sentence; such a word may stand alone and convey a meaning, as contrasted with structure word (q.v.).

fortis consonant

a consonant usually voiceless but characterized by tense and forceful articulation.

free base

any base or stem which is also in itself a word, such as *light.*

free morpheme

a minimum unit of meaning that may either stand alone or combine into compounds and derivatives; in short, it is a word.

free phrase

a group of related words not attached to any particular

environment that may be constructed almost without limit provided the words occur in a normal sequence; all free phrases contain more than one base or base constituent; on the basis of one possible sentence sequence, such as article + adverb + adjective + noun, a vast number of free phrases can be constructed.

frequency

in simplest terms, the number of times a given linguistic feature occurs in a speech community.

fricative

a consonant (sound) produced when the air released by an articulator passes through a narrow aperture with audible friction, as / f v θ ð s š z ž /.

frontal sound

any of several sounds articulated at the front of the tongue, as [e], [c], and [š].

frontal vowels

a group of six vowels usually considered as two series: [i], [e], and [æ] which are relatively long and tense; [I], [ɛ], and [a] which are relatively short and lax. See Appendix D.

full word

a word, in contrast to an empty word (q.v.), which always carries stress, has practical, lexical meaning, may not be omitted from the construction in which it appears, and is taken literally except in figures of speech; in English, full words are nouns, adjectives, verbs, and adverbs.

function

one of the three bases on which classification and analysis

of a language may be founded; also the use of language or its elements in performing an act of communication.

functional meaning

the meaning of a position, that is, of an ordered unit in a construction which can be filled only by certain forms; a minimum free form is a word.

functional shift

the term refers to the process by which words appear as different parts of speech without change in form; thus, *hope* may be a noun or a verb; *hard* may be an adjective or an adverb.

functional varieties

the term refers to classifications of language based upon usage, such as formal, familiar, colloquial, and the like; related to, but not the same as, cultural levels (q.v.).

function nouns

in structural grammar, a sub-class of nouns which are morphemically identical with or closely related to certain noun-determiners, such as *enough, several, some;* which are unchanging in form and so are not inflected; which have no noun-marking suffixes; and which appear in most positions usually filled by nouns.

function verbs

in structural grammar, auxiliaries as standing in place of a full verb phrase, when the full verb has been expressly stated or implied in the immediate context, as when the question, "Are they taking a walk to-day?" brings the reply, "They *will* if they *can*."

function words

any of several groups of words which themselves have

no lexical meaning but serve to indicate various relationships between meaningful words with which they occur, such as prepositions (*of, from, into, etc.*), conjunctions (*and, but*), correlatives (*neither . . . nor*), and negatives (*no, not, etc.*).

fused participle

the *-ing* form of the verb in a structure such as *We heard them calling,* in which the participle cannot indicate a clear distinction between nominal and verbal use as does the variant sentence, *We heard their calling,* in which the participle is clearly of nominal use.

G

generalization

the term refers to a semantic shift, in which the meaning of a word is broadened or extended beyond its original or usual definition and given a far wider application, such as *nice*.

generalized transformations

the term refers to the rules governing combinations which produce compound and complex constructions.

generative grammar

" . . . is a system of explicit rules that assign to each sequence of phones (q.v.), whether of the observed corpus or not, a structural description that contains all the information about the way in which this sequence of phones is represented on each of the several linguistic levels . . . it distinguishes a class of perfectly well-formed (fully-grammatical) sentences." No better brief statement can be offered than this quotation from Noam Chomsky, the scholar most closely associated with generative grammar. A full understanding of this subject can be acquired only by prolonged and detailed study.

gerundive nominal

a transformation of a simple nominal into the possessive form followed by the perfect-tense auxiliary, such as "Mary's having appeared in many plays gave her self-confidence."

glide

a sound of brief duration, a transitional phoneme, produced as the articulators (q.v.), or some of them, make a rapid shift in passing from a semivowel to a true vowel or the reverse.

gloss

a word used to define or identify another word.

glosseme

the term applied to linguistic features that have meaning, and hence includes forms, constructions, and zero elements (q.v.).

glottal stop

a sound produced in the larynx by closing the glottis and then releasing the breath with a slight explosion; not standard in current English.

glottotechnics

that phase of linguistic study which concentrates upon the system of sounds in a language of a given society at a given time.

gradation

the vowel change in sound, not spelling, that results from a shift of stress, as in *democrat, democracy,* where the middle vowel changes from [ə] to [á].

grammar

a description of the ways in which a language uses patterns of structure to convey meaning; it would appear that the term has been used over the years to refer to three different concepts: (a) one view sees grammar as a set of formal patterns by which words are arranged in order to convey meaning; (b) a second view makes grammar a scientific study aimed at the description, analysis, and formalization of language patterns; and (c) a third view holds grammar to be the models of polite usage; more recently there have developed the concepts of structural grammar (q.v.) and transformational (or generative) grammar (q.v.). (For more detailed treatment see Karl W.

Dykema, "Where Our Grammar Came from," in *College English*, Vol. 22, No. 7, April, 1961.)

grammarian

one who studies the use of language as a body of structured forms in order to discover and describe the orderly patterns of arrangement of its various kinds of units.

grammatical analysis

a process whereby one can account for every element in any given sentence; or, in transformational grammar, a procedure for constructing a description of all parts of a given structure.

grammatical deviant

a structure which in some grammatical way departs from normal or customary usage; a grammatical irregularity such as poets often use with striking effect, as simple, for example, as the substituting of one part of speech for another or causing one part of speech to function as a different part.

grammatical markers

terms applied to language structures which classify the role (such as noun, transitive verb, introducer, complement, *etc.*) which the lexical items can play in a sentence.

grammatical structure

morphemes and words organized into a larger meaningful construction; also the process of making such an organization.

grammatical unit

any phonemic or morphemic unit of language which, combined with other such units, comprises a grammatical structure; in another sense, a group of words related to each other in a structure which has a place in the organization of larger structures, as a phrase is part of a sentence.

grapheme

the basic unit of writing in any language; current English has 26 graphemes, that is, the letters of the alphabet, along with their capitals; a grapheme is enclosed in pointed brackets <a>.

graphemics

the spelling practices of a language; also the study of those practices.

graphics

the study of written language in its different forms.

graphonomy

the same as graphics (q.v.).

gravity

a distinctive acoustic feature of English, produced by long oral cavity and small lip apertures, as heard in the muffling on the back vowels / u o ɔ /, the labial consonants / p b m f v /, and the back consonants / h k g ŋ w /.

H

haplology

the loss of one of the two repeated identical sequences in a structure; it is presumed, for example, that there was once the structure, *cod fish fish cakes*, which, by haplology, became *codfish cakes*.

head

the constituent which seems to serve as the center of a construction; it is usually modified by another constituent; the noun, verb, adjective, adverb, and some function words may serve as head; the head has the same grammatical meaning as the whole construction (q.v.).

headed construction

same as endocentric (q.v.).

high vowel

a vowel sounded with the lower jaw relatively closed, as [ee] or [i].

historical linguist

a language scholar whose chief concern is the forms of a language or of languages as existing during one or more eras in history; some are especially concerned with historical change in language forms.

holes

the term refers to irregularities found in the ideolect of an individual or group of them whose speech makes no use of certain sounds which are part of the general pattern of the language; such holes may be found in small-area dialects.

homograph

the correspondence of one word with another in spelling, though never in meaning and not always in pronunciation, as *bow* (a kind of knot), *bow* (to nod or bend), also *bow* (the front part of a ship).

homonymity

the likeness between words or word-elements in sound and sometimes in spelling without likeness in meaning, as he was a *bore;* he hunted the *boar.*

homorganic sounds

two sounds articulated in the same place in the vocal tract, but differing in some other feature, as [d] and [t].

homophonous forms

units of language which are alike in sound.

homophony

the correspondence of one word with another in pronunciation though differing from it in spelling and meaning, as well as origin, as *dear* and *deer* or *meet* and *meat.*

hybrid

a word, part of which is derived from one language and another part from a different language, as beautiful (French and English), churchman (Greek and English).

hyperform

the same as hyperurbanism (q.v.).

hypertagmeme

a grammatical string with features that distinguish it

from other grammatical strings on the same or on different grammatical levels.

hyperurbanism

a usage resulting from the overcorrection of a supposed example of "bad" English, as when a speaker goes from "Him and Jack came in," to "He gave them to Jack and I."

IA method

a term for one of the two approaches to language description used by linguists; IA indicates the method as based on the study of "item" and "arrangement;" the other approach is referred to as IP (q.v.); the IA method describes all forms in a structure as combinations of elements, that is, morphemes and their arrangement. (For details see Andreas Koutsoudas, "The Morpheme Reconsidered," in *International Journal of American Linguistics*, Vol. 29, No. 2, April, 1963.)

idea naming

a relatively modern practice of giving the name of a person to some scientific discovery, an invention, or a philosophical concept, such as *Roentgen rays, pasteurism,* or *bowdlerize.*

ideolect

a distinctive phonemic unit as used by a given speaker which may be slightly different from that used by a different speaker.

ideophonemes

phonemes (sounds) as they occur in the speech or ideolect of individuals, more readily remarked, usually, if possessed of some special idiosyncrasy.

idiom

an expression peculiar to a language, which is not readily understood from either its morphology or its grammatical construction, such as *put off* (postpone) or *at sea* (confused) or *next door* (the adjacent building).

image

a word or group of words which represents a physical or concrete reality which can be experienced through the senses, such as *lake, grass, apple orchard, black felt hat,* as contrasted to what is conceived but not sensed, such as *law, honesty, pragmatic method.*

imagery

in a linguistic rather than a stylistic sense, a method of word formation which utilizes a figure of speech to establish a lexical meaning, as *hothead, long-faced, drifter.*

immediate-constituent grammar

also known as structural grammar, a conception of grammar based on the belief that sentences can be viewed as being made up of two-part constructions on a series of levels; the two main parts of a sentence are its immediate constituents which may be divided and sub-divided until the smallest meaningful units are reached. (For further information, see Charles Carpenter Fries, *The Structure of English: An Introduction to the Construction of English Sentences,* New York, Harcourt, Brace and World, 1952.)

immediate-constituents

See immediate-constituent grammar.

implosive stop

the result of drawing air into the pharynx by closing the vocal cords and pulling the larynx downward to create a slight vacuum above it; when the stop is released, there is a slight movement of air inward, as in [ɒ] and [ɗ].

inchoate aspect

that form of a verb composed of the auxiliary *get* and the

present participle, as *get going, got talking, should get working*.

included clause

a structure with the form of a statement sentence but functioning as a modifier, subject, or complement; similar to the dependent clause of traditional grammar.

included sentence

a type of sentence combination in which a transform of one sentence occupies a position within another sentence, as in *I bought a boat designed by him*, in which *a boat* is in the object range of *I bought*, but it is also in the subject range of *designed by him*.

includer

a function word to signal an included clause; such words include *after, although, because, only, since,* and many more, as well as the relative pronouns.

indirect object

the first nominal complement in a transitive construction, having two complements which can be transformed into a prepositional phrase, usually with *to* or *for*, as "He mailed me the book." (He mailed the book *to* me.)

infinitival nominal

an infinitive form which may appear (a) as subject of a copulative sentence, (b) as object of one of a restricted class of verbs, or (c) in adverbials of purpose following *for*, as in
   (a) For Jill *to remember* is difficult.
   (b) My friend begged me *to drive* carefully.
   (c) I brought this hat for you *to wear*.

infixed differentials

morphemes which are in neither initial nor terminal position and which are different from each other, though the morphemes before and after are alike or closely similar, as *sip, sap, sop, sup,* or *strip, strap, stripe.*

inflected

the term indicating a characteristic of some languages in that certain words have different forms to show variation in meaning and in relation to each other and to other words, such as the several cases of nouns or the persons and tenses of verbs.

inflection

also called inflectional ending, the bound morpheme used to indicate the grammatical function of a word, as the genitive or possessive case of a noun is indicated by the *'s* in *man's* or the plural is indicated by the *es* in *campuses.*

inflectional variants

the term refers to the alterations in the forms of words which indicate changes in meaning and relationship, such as *boy* (one), *boys* (more than one).

information

in a linguistic sense, the meaning transmitted by a set of previously-arranged signals (language units) of which the minimum possible is two, so that the amount of information increases as the number of alternative signals increases. (For a detailed discussion, see George A. Miller, "What Is Information Measurement?" in *The American Psychologist,* Vol. 8, January, 1953.)

initial string

in transformational grammar, the first element in a derivation which consists of a series of sequences or lines, such
as $S \rightarrow NP + VP$; see intermediate string and terminal
string.

inner complement

in structural grammar, the third position in a sentence or
clause of four-position construction, regarded as the major
method of syntactic positioning in English; usually the
indirect object (q.v.) of traditional grammar.

input string

in a transformation, that one of a pair of constructions
which is altered to produce the other, as the first statement
below:

The girl came home.   *The girl did not come home.*

intensity

the strength or force of the meaning of a word; there
appears to be a constant tendency to find new intensive
terms, and this may account for the popularity (perhaps
only a fad) of such words as *fabulous, terrific,* and words
(some lately-coined) with the prefix {*super-*}; note the
language of current advertising.

interaction of words

the influence which words have upon each other in a given
construction, the result of which is context, to which one
looks for clues in selecting the fitting definition of a mul-
tiple-meaning word.

interdental

a dentilingual consonant produced with the tip of the
tongue placed between the teeth, / θ ð /.

intermediate strings

in transformational grammar, the series of lines, made up of elements connected by plus signs, which are found in a derivation between the initial string and the terminal string (q.v.).

internal contour

the pattern of pitch established by either of the two types of close juncture (q.v.): the optional / | / produces the internal contour /2/ — /2/; obligatory / || / produces the internal contour /2/ ↗ /2/.

internal modification

a morphological process in which a change of function and/or meaning is indicated by a phonemic replacement within a word, such as *swam* for the past tense of *swim* and *teeth* for the plural of *tooth*.

internal reconstruction

the use of internal evidence, such as the identification of allomorphs, in support of inferences about an earlier stage of a language.

interposed object

the object is called interposed when it occurs between the two parts of a composite verb (q.v.), as in "His father sent *him* away."

interrogative morpheme

the morpheme in terminal place in a statement which receives a decided rising inflection, thus giving the statement the force of a question, such as

The cat has eaten the c a n a r y

interruption

a distinctive acoustic feature of English characterized by the momentary obstruction of the flow of breath, as in the voiceless stops / p t k c / and the voiced obstruents / b d g j /.

intonation

the interrelationship or interaction in a given utterance of pitch, juncture, prolongation, and pacing.

intonation-pattern

the particular arrangement of variations in pitch (q.v.) which are recognizable in an utterance of a given speaker, and which are indications of meaning.

intransitive construction

a structure in which there occurs one of a class of verbs which cannot be followed by a nominal or an adjective in the third position in a sentence of the form: Nom + V + Pred + Adv. Some such verbs may occur with or without an adverb; others must be followed by an adverb of location or motion.

intrasubjective synonymy

the degree to which a language unit, usually a word, carries the same meaning for all members of a speech community, that is to say, that the synonyms are joined for each subject by sameness of stimulus meaning (q.v.).

introducer

a word or word sequence which may appear before any sentence proper, often referring to time, place, or circumstance though not necessarily; some examples are: *In a moment* she will come through that door. *At this point* his speech caused excited laughter. *There* came a great shout from the crowd.

inversion

in structural grammar, the method of forming a question by reversing the positions of the subject and first auxiliary of a statement, as *she has arrived* becomes *has she arrived?*

IP method

one of the two approaches to language description used by linguists; IP indicates "item" and "process;" the other approach is referred to as IA (q.v.); the IP method describes most forms as derived from certain base forms.

isochronism

a feature of English whereby the amount of time between two primary stresses tends to be the same, regardless of the amount of material that happens to be between them; this feature is clearly related to juncture (q.v.); note the following:

Swimming / is difficult #
Swimming / is very difficult #
The swimming lesson / was very difficult #

isogloss

a line drawn on a map by a dialect linguist to mark the outer boundaries or limits of the area in which a regionally distributed feature may be found.

isomorphic systems

the term is used to describe a situation in which one linguistic system, the writing system, for instance, represents a related system, such as the phonological system, so perfectly that every important feature of each system has its counterpart in the other.

J

juncture

the transition from one speech utterance to the next by either a catch in or a stoppage of the breath, thus establishing a mark of grammatical boundaries; English has four junctures, one open and three close.

K

kernel sentence

in generative grammar, one of a group of sentences which are simple, active, and declarative, and from which all other sentences may be derived by transformations.

L

labial sound

consonant sounds articulated or modified by the lips, as / p b m w /.

labiodental sound

a sound articulated with the lower lip and the upper front teeth, as / f / or / v /.

lateral sound

the sound of the consonant / l / articulated while the mouth is closed by contact of the tip of the tongue against the gums, leaving an opening at one or both sides.

law of concatenation

a law by which linguistic elements in a string (q.v.) may be gathered together according to any system of syntax, but their order may not be changed.

laxness

a distinctive acoustic feature of English characterized by relative relaxation of the tongue and jaw while in the act of articulation.

lax phoneme

a sound made with tongue and jaw relatively relaxed, as in the simple vowels / i ɫ u e з o æ a ɔ / and the voiced consonants / b m v o d z n l r j ž g y ŋ w /.

lax vowel

a vowel which permits some degree of relaxation of the tongue and mouth parts as compared to other vowels, as / i / compared to / u /.

layer of structure

an isolated utterance, or the immediate constituents of a structure, as *Good Doctor Tom* as one layer; *Good* and *Doctor* and *Tom* as the next layer.

lenis consonant

a consonant usually voiced but pronounced with relatively little tension of the organs of articulation, as / b d g /.

lexical contamination

a term applied to a mixed or blended status of a given phonetic change found in an area between two areas which give clear evidence of the change, so that one construction is contaminated by another, such as, through the confusion of *consist of* with *comprise,* the form *comprise of.*

lexical meaning

the meaning of a morpheme or word standing alone, apart from any meaning which it may acquire by reason of its position in some larger structure; more simply, the "dictionary meaning."

lexical units

a class of linguistic forms made up of movable segments whose meaning cannot be deduced from a knowledge of its parts and the way they are put together, such as *court martial;* another view sees the lexical unit as that unit in a speech signal that conveys to the listener the intention of the speaker.

lexicon

the actual words which are represented by symbols in a transformation, commonly listed below a given transformation; in another sense, it is the total stock of morphemes in any language.

lexiostatistics

the study of two or more languages of the same family to determine, by comparison of certain words or forms, when the member languages separated from the parent language and/or from each other.

ligature

a grapheme formed by combining two letters or characters, such as / fl / or / ou /.

limitation

the opposite of extension (q.v.), that is, a word may lose one or another of its meanings which no longer apply usefully.

linguals

a term suggested as a substitute for the term liquids in reference to the consonants /l / and / r / since they are paired by their lingual qualities.

linguistic borrowing

the adoption into a given language of a word or dialect feature from another language foreign to it, often to fill a perceived need.

linguistic community

the same as speech community (q.v.).

linguistic substitution

the use by a speaker or writer of a foreign language of a feature of his native speech in place of some feature of that foreign language.

liquid

a term applied to the vowel-like consonants that are produced without friction /l r /.

live suffix

a suffix such as {-able} or {-ity}, which can be added to a great many verbs, thus giving rise to many new coinages.

loan-shift

a type of borrowing by one language from another which substitutes native morphemes for some of those in the imported word.

loan-translation

a word taken into a language from the translation of a word in another language, as English *storm-trooper* was acquired from the German.

loan-word

a word "borrowed" in its entirety from another language with no change in meaning and, usually, none in spelling, as *soprano* from the Italian, *siesta* from the Spanish, *chauffeur* from the French, and the like.

localism

the peculiar usage or pronunciation of a word which is characteristic of the speech of a particular geographic area; a regionalism.

locution

a verbal expression or the manner of its delivery, usually as occurring in various social situations.

logogram

a grapheme, not itself a word, which stands for a complete word, such as the system used to specify moves in the game of chess.

logographic

the term refers to a system of writing in which each word is represented by a symbol or logogram (q.v.).

long vowel

a complex vowel formed by uniting a simple vowel with one of the offset glides (q.v.) / y w h / and pronounced as one vocalic cluster, as in the case of / aw / of *mouse*; in a general sense, any vowel may be called long when lengthened by the prolongation of its articulation.

loss of intensity

a weakening or fading in the meaning of a word, said to result from a human tendency to exaggerate, so that words such as *dreadful, horrible, awful, awfully* no longer carry the force and strength of meaning which they once conveyed.

low vowel

a vowel sounded with the lower jaw relatively wide open, as [aw].

M

macron

a line drawn over a vowel to show that it is long; no significant use is made of it in current English.

macrotagmeme

the top layer, or tagmeme of a sentence type, which is the composite picture of the basic taxemes (q.v.) of an isolated utterance.

mapping

an application of mathematical set theory in which a series of integers is coupled with elements of an alphabet into sequences.

marking

a characteristic of the use of English verbs by which to indicate the presence of a certain restriction upon their meaning; markers may include: inflections, the auxiliaries, the *to* of the infinitive, applied so that the tense, person, number, mood, and voice of a verb may be indicated.

mass/abstract noun

in transformational grammar, a noun similar to the traditional abstract noun, which cannot be preceded by a cardinal number; such expressions as *two pieties, three happinesses,* are not considered acceptable.

matched sentences

a sequence of at least two sentences, both of which contain the same words in all but one or two positions, as "Some people vacation in the summer. Some vacation in the winter. Some vacation in a different season each year." It is clear that the first and second sentences are better matched than is either the first or the second with the third sentence.

material meaning

a meaning which is regarded as basic, essential, substantial, central, as opposed to what is relative or peripheral.

mathematical linguistics

the investigation of the underlying structure of language in an effort to work out the basic general laws of structure in language.

matrix

a charted or listed method of representing the number of times that cognates appear in different members of the same language family.

matrix sentence

in transformational grammar, a basic sentence, known in traditional grammar as an independent clause, into which other structures may be embedded.

mechano-linguistics

that aspect of linguistics which involves the use of computers and computer science in linguistic analysis.

median sound

the sound produced when the oral passage is open at the mid-line, as in /r/, /y/, and /w/.

mellowness

a distinctive acoustic feature of English, characterized by a muffling of the friction in the spirants / θ ð /.

metalinguistics

the linguistic study concerned with the interrelationship of linguistics with other cultural factors in a society.

metaphor

a category of semantic change by which a word takes on new applications by reason of metaphoric resemblances, as the names for the parts of the body have been applied in *the head of a nail, an arm of the sea* (a bay), *leg of a table, foot of the hill, etc.*

metathesis

the morphological process of the transposition of letters, syllables, or sounds within a word by which, for example, the Old English *hwale* became the modern *whale*.

methodics

a term indicating the techniques and processes involved when linguistics becomes a subject for classroom teaching; used chiefly by British linguists; to be distinguished from methodology.

microlinguistic meaning

the term refers to the identity or difference in meaning which results when a part of a larger structure is replaced by a different part.

mid vowel

a vowel sounded with the jaw approximately half-open, as [ɛ] or [e].

minimal pairs

words which differ from each other by only one phoneme, and no two words can differ from each other by less, such as *pill* and *fill,* *bet* and *pet, jab* and *tab.*

modal

a type of auxiliary indicating that an assertion is in some way qualified or tentative, such as *shall, will, can, may,* and the like.

modification

the influence of one constituent or construction upon another by a limitation or specification.

modifier

the constituent which exercises a limiting or specifying influence over another; as to meaning, a modifier may not stand alone; in another sense, a modifier is one of the two components (the other being a head) in a structure of modification (q.v.).

monogenetic theory

in linguistics, the theory that all of the world's languages originated in a single source.

morph

in its simplest sense, the term is applied to an indivisible unit of meaning; any morph is a phoneme (q.v.) or a pattern of phonemes, but a phoneme is a morph only if it carries meaning.

morpheme

one view holds the morpheme to be the basic unit of meaning in a language, with English displaying three kinds of morphemes: the bound phonemic (the /z/ of possession in *Mary's*), the bound syllabic (the {-*ly*} of adverbial function in *quickly*), and free word simple (*Mary* and *quick*); another notion sees the morpheme as one of a class of parts of speech which includes prefixes, suffixes, the inflectional endings, and other elements such as those that form the past participle or an interrogative or produce emphasis (the transformational view); still another view holds that the morpheme is that unit of grammar the arrangement of which is specified by the syntax, and the resulting sequences of which are used to predict the physical form of utterance. (Note: a definition of this term has been the subject of debate by linguists for more than twenty-five years.)

morpheme alternants

the term applied to a situation in which a word has two stems corresponding to two forms of the word, for example, the singular and the plural, or the nominative and the genitive, and the like; another view holds that when expressions in a given language are reduced to the smallest sequence of phonemes which can be considered to have the same meaning, such resulting parts are morpheme alternants.

morpheme word

the minimum unit of free meaning in a language; morpheme and word boundaries coincide to form one simple unit of meaning, such as *dog*.

morphemics

the identification and possible combinations of phonemes and their use in the organization of meaningful groups called morphs (q.v.).

morphograms

unchanging representations of the same morphemes, regardless of morphophonemic variations in the spoken language, as {-ed} is always the sign of the past tense of all weak verbs.

morphographemic rules

the general rules governing writing.

morphographic combination

an instance of a morpheme which has two allomorphs (q.v.), both of which are represented by the same spelling, as the two allomorphs of the prefix {con-}, /kən/ and /kan/, are both represented by the morphographic combination <con>.

morphographic writing

also called morphemic writing, it is a writing system which has a separate symbol for each morpheme, such as the Chinese; a limited amount of such writing is found in English, most of it in special fields, as phonetics, punctuation, proof-reading.

morphological marks

the general term for the punctuation marks taken collectively.

morphological process

the term refers to any method of word formation, such as compounding, affixing, or telescoping, and the like.

morphology

the study of forms of language, especially the different forms used in declensions, conjugations, and wordbuilding.

morphophonemic analysis

the study of a language in order to identify and describe its phonemes and morphemes and the ways in which they function in relation to each other.

81

morphophonemic change

a change of allomorphs connected with verb tenses and participial forms, such as the change of the vowel in the stem to form the past tense of certain verbs, such as *ride, rode.*

morphophonemics

the study of the alternation of phonemes (q.v.) within a morpheme (q.v.) and the description of phonemes as constituents of morphemes.

morphophonetic rules

the general rules governing pronunciation.

morphotactics

that phase of linguistics which is concerned with the characteristic structure of morphs and morphemes occurring in sequences in a language.

muffling

the deadening of articulation by use of the oral cavity, the lips, or the dental ridge which is responsible for the English acoustic features of gravity (q.v.) and mellowness (q.v.).

N

narrow nuclei

a term often applied to the complex vowels formed by the use of the offset glides (q.v.) / y w /, which constrict both the oral cavity and the lip aperture.

nasal release

the release of sound through the nose rather than through the mouth when a stop is followed by a nasal; indicated by the diacritic [ᴺ] following the consonant.

nasals

sounds produced when the oral passage is completely stopped but there is free passage for air through the nasal cavity and the nostrils; there are three nasals in English: the bilabial [m], the apico-alveolar [n], and the dorso-velar [ŋ].

nasality

a distinctive acoustic feature of English, characterized by use of the nose in phonemic formation and articulation.

neologism

a general term for any new word introduced into the language regardless of the method of its creation—by derivation, compounding, telescoping, or whatever.

nodes

the term designating those points in a branching tree diagram (q.v.) which are represented by dots.

noeme

the meaning of a glosseme (q.v.).

nominal

a transformed adjective or verb form related to and functioning as a noun; in addition, noun clauses, infinitive phrases, gerund phrases, and personal pronouns may stand in nominal positions.

nominalization morpheme

a bound morpheme which, used as suffix, indicates a word that will function as a noun, as {-ness}, {-ite}, {-ist}, {-ment}, etc. See nominal.

nominalizations

the various ways of creating nominals (q.v.).

nominal phrase

a word of noun function but having two bases rather than one, as *loudspeaker* or *fountainhead* as compared to *tree* or *horse*.

nomenclature

a body of names or terms, to some degree systematized, associated with a particular field of human activity, such as journalism, education, a science, an art, or the like.

nonce-word

a new word produced by a single speaker only, in some special situation, or on a special occasion, which may never be used again or by a few associates for a short time.

non-contrastive distribution

the same as complementary distribution (q.v.).

non-headed construction

the same as exocentric (q.v.).

non-sequential morphemes

a string of morphemes which occurs without containing a plus juncture, so that a cut (q.v.) must be made on some other ground; an example is the word *division*.

non-syllabic

a phoneme which occurs as all or part of the onset (q.v.) or the coda (q.v.) of a phonemic syllable.

non-vocoid

a term suggested for use in phonetics as a substitute for the term consonant, while vocoid would substitute for the term vowel.

notation

the term refers to linguistic transcriptions, such as the symbols which represent categories of sound or grammatical categories.

noun determiners

a group of function words which are the most common noun-making signals which precede the nouns they mark, either immediately or with certain types of words coming between; morphologically, the most common noun-determiners are pronouns.

nounform

a structural unit which functions as a nominal.

noun in apposition

the same as appositive (q.v.).

noun of quantity

a noun, indicative of amount, which functions with *of* as a determiner, as *a quart of milk, a gallon of paint.*

noun phrase

a structural unit which functions as the "subject" of a kernel sentence in transformational grammar, and symbolized as $S \to NP + VP$.

nuclear sound

a vowel sound, always the most prominent sound in the syllable in which it occurs.

nucleus

the most prominent phone in a syllable; also called syllabic (q.v.).

O

obligatory internal close juncture

the suprasegmental phoneme (q.v.) of transition, symbolized by / ‖ /, which discriminates phrasal and clausal boundaries and calls for punctuation; in English, this juncture (q.v.) is usually accompanied by the internal contour /2/ ↗ /2/.

obligatory terminal close juncture

the suprasegmental phoneme of transition, symbolized by /#/, which discriminates sentence boundaries and calls for punctuation; in English, this juncture (q.v.) is accompanied by either one of the terminal contours: /3/ — /1/ or /3/ — /4/.

observation sentence

an occasion sentence (q.v.) which elicits assent or dissent, depending upon the stimulus meaning (q.v.) which the sentence conveys to the hearer.

obstruent

the term refers to the voiced stops in English / b d g j /, which obstruct the breath stream without stopping it.

occasion sentence

a statement made in connection with, or prompted by, an immediately observable circumstance, out of which comes the stimulus that results in assent or dissent on the part of the hearer.

offset glide

any one of the three semivowels of transition / y w h / used after a vowel to make a complex nucleus of a syllable.

onset

that part of a phonemic syllable which precedes the peak (q.v.).

onset glide

any one of the three semivowels of transition / y w h / used before a vowel, as in pursuit / pŭr - syut /.

opaque word

a word whose meaning is not immediately apparent to the average reader, such as scientific terms with classical roots, such as *megaton, pyrogenic, polyphonic.*

open classes

classes made up of nouns, verbs, adjectives, or adverbs, because their total membership may be changed from time to time by the addition of new words or the dropping of old words.

open juncture

the suprasegmental phoneme of transition / + / that establishes morphemic and word boundaries on stressed elements, as in *this + page*; this juncture (q.v.) is open because it does not interrupt the flow of speech and does not call for punctuation.

open transition

the short pause required when two successive phonemes must be articulated with distinct separateness in order to avoid misreading, such as *an - aim* to distinguish from *a - name.*

optional internal close juncture

the suprasegmental phoneme of transition, symbolized by

/ |/, which discriminates the word-group boundaries with-out any need for punctuation; this juncture (q.v.) is usually accompanied by the internal contour /2/ — /2/.

orality

a distinctive acoustic feature of English which is character-ized by articulation in the oral cavity only, with no use made of the nasal passage.

orders

groups into which morphemes are classified, mutually ex-clusive and occupying definable places in the sequence of morphemes forming a word.

orthography

the study of a system of spelling or of spelling practices according to a standard of usage; also the process of identification of phonemes, or the distinctive vowels and consonants, of a language.

outer complement

in transformational grammar, this term indicates the num-ber 4 position in the four-position syntax of English, usually denoting the direct object in a sentence in the active voice.

output string

in a transformation, that one of a pair of constructions which results from an alteration of the other, as the second sentence below:
The girl came home.   *The girl did not come home.*

P marker

phrase marker, a representation of an immediate constituent structure for a string, such as the branching tree
type of diagram.

pacing

the speed of speech delivery as determined by the intonational habits or practices of the speaker.

palatal

the term applied to a consonantal phoneme produced by
placing the front (but not the tip) of the tongue against
or very near the hard palate; in English these would
be /h k g y/.

paradigm

a means of displaying the inflectional forms of a word
or class of words in an orderly fashion, as is customary in
listing a declension or a conjugation.

paradigmatic

the term refers to the pattern method of representing the
changes in forms occasioned by different environments.

paralanguage

a system of non-phonemic articulations which, however, do
manage to convey some sense of meaning or semantic
value; a pseudo-language, such as a small child's babbling
or an adult's groans, sighs, and similar sounds.

parataxis

the terms refers to the syntax involved in constructions

of coordination, especially without the use of conjunctions, as *we met, we spoke, we parted.*

particularizer

one of a small group of words which may appear in a noun phrase between a quantifier (q.v.) and the adjective, including *certain, other, particular.*

past participle morpheme

that element which, added to the base form of the verb, produces the past participle form; in the case of regular verbs, the added morpheme is {-*ed*}; among the irregular verbs, some have a base form and past participle form which are identical, as *put* and *hit;* so-called "strong verbs" undergo vowel change in the stem or other change in the base to form the past participle, as in *ride, rode; buy, bought; say, said; build, built; etc.*

pattern grammar

a theory of grammar which holds that language may be analyzed and described in terms of pattern both phonological and morphological.

peak

the central necessary part, or nucleus, of a phonemic syllable which must always be present, while the other two parts of the syllable, onset and coda (q.v.), may or may not be present.

pejoration

a worsening of the meaning of a word, the opposite of amelioration (q.v.), as *silly,* which once meant *happy,* now means *foolish.*

perfectivizing prefix

a morpheme which serves, not to express a meaning, but rather a distinction in meaning, as in *disinter, reinter,* wherein the prefixes {dis-} and {re-} indicate two distinct applications of the word *inter.*

permitted strings

in generative grammar, this term denotes the direct grammatical representations of the permitted sentences (strings, q.v.) of a language.

permutation

in transformational grammar, a rule symbolized as $a + b \rightarrow b + a$, as in the derivation of *Here came Mary* from *Mary came here;* in a more general application, the term refers to a change in the meaning of a word, as *bead* once meant *prayer, wan* once meant *dark.* See semantic shift.

phase

any part of an utterance in a series of perceptible articulations.

phatic function

the function of language when used for purposes of polite sociability, often called "small talk" or "chit-chat."

phone

a minimum unit of speech sound, that is, a minimal segment of the stream of speech; these units or segments are organized by groups into phonemes (q.v.).

phoneme

the simplest unit of sound; in a specific utterance, a particular phoneme may be represented by a certain specific sound, while in another utterance the same phoneme may be represented by a slightly different sound.

phoneme of juncture

a suprasegmental phoneme (q.v.) used as a means of transition or moving from one structure of linguistic material to another.

phonemic

relative to or based upon the phonemes of a given language.

phonemic morpheme

a bound morpheme (q.v.) on the phonemic rather than the syllable level, as the /z/ of possession in *Tom's* or the /s/ of the plural *birds*.

phonemic transcription

a method of writing in which all phonemes are represented, each by a single grapheme or symbol; a given phoneme or a given group of phonemes is placed between single slash lines, / /.

phonemics

the study of that branch of linguistics which is concerned with the identification and description of the phonemes of a language.

phonestheme patterning

a graphic representation of forms which are interrelated through rhyme or assonance, such as, very briefly,
    act
    fact
    pact   past
                part   pert

phonetic alternation

the term refers to the situation wherein a phoneme in a construction may alternate with another phoneme according to environment.

phonetic change

a change in the sound of a phoneme such as is encountered in different dialects of the same language; also a sound change to be noted in a form, having taken place between one historical period and a later period.

phonetic intensives

kinds of sound symbolism, found chiefly in poetry and other literary works, which include speech sounds that imitate actual sounds (onomatopoeia), speech sounds arranged to make them easy or difficult to utter, and speech sounds which suggest meaning.

phonetics

the branch of linguistics dealing with the analysis, description, and classification of speech sounds, including both the physiological process, or articulation, and the physical attributes, or acoustics; the study of the system of sounds in a language with more refined description than the phonemes.

phonetic transcription

a method of writing, using a phonetic alphabet, in which a separate character or symbol is used for every distinguishable type of speech sound.

phonological construction

any construction in which phonemes are put together according to the language's rules of combination based on the nature of the language; in English, there are certain combinations never encountered, such as initial /mb/ or terminal /tp/.

phonological criteria

the rules by which data concerning the sounds of a language may be systematized; also the rules for the classing of allophones into phonemes.

phonological system

the regularities of the sound features of a language, both phonetic and phonemic, as represented by the various diagrams, listings, and classifications devised to outline aspects of the system.

phonological word

a construction existing only in the phonological system but which is not necessarily either a lexical or a graphic word; an example is found in the way in which some people pronounce the middle part of the expression, *did you go?*— the /di:ju/ in the expression is a phonological word.

phonologist

a linguist whose special concern is the study of the sound system of a language. See phonology and phonological system.

phonology

the study of the system that controls the use of the sounds in speech; the units of the system are phonemes (q.v.); in other words, the study of phonetics and phonemics together in the history of the sound changes that have occurred in the evolution of a language.

phonotactics

that phase of phonemics which is especially concerned with the structural characteristics of phonemic sequences; phonotactical description defines the phoneme classes which occur in a language.

phrase

referred to in linguistics as a non-minimum free form, an utterance that may stand alone but which is phonemically divisible; another view calls a phrase as much of an utterance as is spoken between two clearly distinguishable pauses or terminal junctures (q.v.).

phrase-formative

one of the special assumptions of Leonard Bloomfield, namely, that a phrase may contain a bound form that is not part of a word, and such a form is a phrase-formative; his example is the possessive [z] in *the man I saw yesterday's daughter*. (See Leonard Bloomfield, "A Set of Postulates for the Science of Language," in *Language*, Vol. II, Linguistic Society of America, 1926.)

phrase-structure rule

in transformational grammar, a stated instruction to replace one symbol by one or more different symbols, utilizing an arrow, as in
$$NP_p \rightarrow T + N + Z_2;$$
in more general terms, one of several formation rules that govern the construction of the immediate constituents (q.v.) of a kernel sentence (q.v.).

pitch

the term refers to tone accent; the intonation heights of spoken communication; English is characterized by four degrees of pitch, the suprasegmental phonemes /4/ (highest), /3/ (high), /2/ (normal), and /1/ (low).

pitch contours

the typical patterns of transition from one intonation segment to another, such as the terminal contour of high-falling /3/ − /1/ or the internal contour of normal-rising /2/ ↗ /2/.

pitch phonemes

the term refers to the four recognized levels of pitch (q.v.), especially to the slight variations in pitch from one syllable to another which have some influence upon meaning.

plateau

a term applied to the sustaining of the highest pitch in a structure in which the plateau rises from a syllable with secondary pitch, which occurs before the primary, and continues to the primary, as in 2   3   3 1
"She's going to the movies."

plosive

the same as stop (q.v.).

plural morpheme

in transformational grammar, a morpheme, symbolized by $\{Z_2\}$, which, when added to a concrete noun, changes that noun from a singular to a plural; the plural morpheme takes one of the following forms: {-s}, {-es}, {-en}, and {∅}, the last when singular and plural are the same, as *deer*.

plurisegmental features

the term refers to stress, pitch, and general quality as the language features which make possible the continuous overlapping of articulation which extends over stretches of various lengths in individual speech.

plus juncture

also called "open juncture," it is one form of transition between sounds, or to put it another way, it marks a boundary between sounds; symbolized by /+/, it always occurs between secondary stresses, and between secondary and primary stresses unless one of the other junctures is present there; it does not call for punctuation, usually appearing in such instances as *I + scream* as distinguished from *ice + cream,* or *a + nail* from *an + ale.*

point of articulation

any one of the articulators (q.v.) which is used with some degree of passage of air to produce a sound; the principal points are the upper lip, the upper teeth, the alveolar ridge, the palate, and the velum.

polysemes

the multiple meanings acquired or possessed by a word.

polysemy

the condition of words which have multiple meanings, such as *wit, bore, cut.*

portmanteau

a word, usually taken humorously, which is formed by telescoping parts of two distinct words; a number of classic examples are to be found in Lewis Carroll's "Jabberwocky."

position (as a noun)

in structural grammar, a construction is conceived of as a group of ordered units, each of which is a position and can be filled only by certain forms; the term also refers to the "place" in a construction occupied by a unit.

positional grammar

a concept of grammar which holds that linguistic analysis may be based on the belief that an English construction is made up of ordered units, each of which is a position (q.v.).

post-apical

the term which describes those consonants articulated just behind the tip of the tongue, as / c š j ž /.

postbase

a morpheme which normally follows a base but may follow another postbase and, being without the restrictions of suffixes, may be used to build constructions containing them with great freedom, as shown by such a word as *conversationalistic*, which includes four postbases.

postdeterminer

one of a class of words which follow the regular determiners (q.v.) and which precede the adjectives, and include ordinal numbers, cardinal numbers, comparatives, and superlatives, as the *first* day, the past *several* hours, any *more* time, the *fewest* red apples.

post-modifier

in structural grammar, any modifier of a noun or noun cluster used as subject which has a position following the subject.

postphrase

a morpheme that is inflectionally bound to a phrase, often occurring in the so-called group genitive, as the {z} in *the late Queen of England's consort*.

postverbal phrase

a phrase usually composed of adjectivals (q.v.) occurring in a position after the verb or verbal material, although the phrase may occur before the verb in another construction; as a postverbal phrase it would appear, for example, as in "This gem is *a fine old stone.*"

prearticle

in transformational grammar, one of a small class of words which can precede articles or demonstratives or genitives, and the zero article; the most common of these are *all, only, both,* and *just,* as in *all* the pups, *only* that girl, *both* these men, *just* my luck, *all* {ø} women.

prebase

a morpheme which is morphologically bound in that it does not occur alone, but it is not bound phonologically; the prebase is usually initial and is joined to a base which is rarely found to combine in this way with some other morpheme, as in the case of *svelte,* that is, / s + vélt /.

predeterminer

in transformational grammar, a constituent which precedes both regular and postdeterminers (q.v.) in a string; a predeterminer is always followed by the word *of,* as in *all of* the books, *some of* the plants, *each of* my friends.

predeterminer morpheme

in transformational grammar, the term applied to the word *of* which always follows a predeterminer (q.v.).

predicate

one, usually the second, of the two immediate constituents (q.v.) in a structure of predication (q.v.), consisting of a verb alone or a verb followed by a complement of some kind; the term comes out of traditional grammar but is still used by some modern linguists.

predicatival

a verb consisting of an *-ing* form which does not vary according to the form of the subject, hence similar to the present participial phrase of traditional grammar; the term also applies to the verbal material in a subjectless sentence, such as *Be a good boy;* this verb form may also be complex.

predicator

the verb or verbal material whose form is selected or designated by the subject for the sake of agreement or concord; this form may also be complex.

prefix

a bound morpheme which never stands alone, but always precedes the base (q.v.) to which it is bound, as the {*con-*} in *conduct.*

prefixal meaning

that aspect of the meaning of a word which is imparted by the presence of a prefix, as {*pre-*} (before), {*post-*} (after), {*sub-*} (under), and the like.

pre-modifier

in structural grammar, any modifier of a noun or noun cluster used as subject which has a position preceding the subject.

prescriptivism

a term applied to traditional grammar, referring to its tendency to evaluate usage and set down rules as to what is "good" or "bad" English.

presentence element

a morpheme shifted into first position, thus creating a yes/no interrogative, or a morpheme in first position when a statement is transformed into a question not of a yes/no type, as
Can we go skating to-day?
Who is arriving this afternoon?
When will the car be delivered?

preverb

an auxiliary verb when it is moved to first position in a sentence, thus transforming a statement into a yes/no question, as *Will* the senator run for office again? or *Has* he been driving in races for many years?

pre-verbal adverb

that variety of adverb which takes a position in front of the main verb and follows the auxiliary, if any, and the noun subject; these adverbs may be positive, such as *always, surely, fortunately, etc.*, or negative, such as *never, hardly, seldom,* and the like.

process of subtraction

See back-formation.

productive affix

any prefix or suffix which, when attached to an existing word, thereby produces a new word, such as *entrain, deplane, imaginativeness.*

PRO forms

in transformational grammar, a simplified technique for plotting transformations in which PRO_d stands for the PRO form of determiner, such as *some,* and PRO_n stands for the PRO form of nouns, such as *one, body,* or *thing.*

102

prolongation

the lengthening or stretching of a sound in a spoken syllable of maximum stress for purposes of emphasis, as in *Donnn't do it!*

proportional analogy

the term refers to the process of analogy by which an unknown form may be postulated on the basis of known forms, as *dog* : *dogs* = *hog* : X, the unknown, which is thus shown to be *hogs*; another view would use this term to describe an adaptation (q.v.) which replaces one alternant (q.v.) with another.

protophoneme

a phoneme regarded as a "prototype" or model of corresponding phonemes in other languages which are referred to as reflexes of the protophoneme usually marked by an asterisk; the result is a line in a matrix, as

IE	Greek	Latin	Sanscrit	English
*p	p	p	p	f

psycholinguistics

the study of the interrelationships between psychological principles and data and those of linguistics.

Q

qualifier

a constituent which customarily modifies an adjective, for example, *very* or *quite*, that is, one of a group of function words indicating the degree to which the meaning of the adjective it appears with is applicable; qualifiers also appear, though less commonly, with adverbs.

quantifier

a modifier in a noun phrase which stands between the determiner (q.v.) and the first adjective, if there is one, including such words as *few* and *many* and all the numbers.

quasi-transformation

an instance in which two constructions fall short of fulfilling the conditions for a transformation, as when the domain of transformation is smaller than a sentence, as in *give him this*, *give this to him*, neither structure is a sentence; or when a transformation specifies for one of its components a class rather than an individual morpheme.

question tag

an interrogative structure added to a statement, giving it an interrogative value and at the same time indicating that an affirmative or negative reply is expected, as

"My friend isn't here to-day, is he?" (aff. tag).

"My friend is here to-day, isn't he?" (neg. tag).

The entire interrogative structure is often called a tag question.

radiation

a category of semantic change by which the meaning of a word broadens along several lines to include different but related things, as the word *paper* once applied only to writing sheets of cotton, linen, or other fibers, but is now applied as well to a variety of things written on paper, such as an essay, a treatise, a dissertation, a lecture, an article, *etc.*

range

See distribution.

reciprocal assimilation

that type of assimilation (q.v.) in which two consecutive sounds influence each other to produce a compromise between the two, as [dj] is often made into [dʒ] in such words as *during* or *education*, or as /n/ becomes /ŋ/ before /k/ or /g/.

recursiveness

in transformational grammar, a property of grammar which permits the optional embedding of a constituent sentence (q.v.) after any noun in a matrix sentence (q.v.), thus making a grammar capable of producing an infinite number of sentences.

reduction

in transformational grammar, a rule symbolized as a + b → c, as in the derivation *I see that Mary has returned* from the two kernel sentences (q.v.), *I see* and *Mary has returned*.

redundancy

in linguistics, the difference between the total theoretical communicative capacity of a language (a variety of code) and the average amount of information (q.v.) conveyed, hence, the unused capacity of a language. (For further details, see H. A. Gleason, Jr., *An Introduction to Descriptive Linguistics*, Rev. ed., New York, Holt, Rinehart, and Winston, 1961, Chap. 23.)

reduplication

a morphological process of English in which the doubling of a word, usually with some internal change, creates an echoing emphasis, as in *namby-pamby, twiddle-twaddle, razzle-dazzle*.

referent

the actual object, relationship, *etc.*, in the outside world that is referred to by a word.

referential meaning

the term refers to lexical meaning, the denotation of a word, as contrasted to structural or differential meaning (q.v.).

reflex

a form which has developed from another (earlier) form.

regionalism

a variety of speech, distinct from dialect, which is characteristic of a rather large geographical area and which does not hinder communication, although within the region a number of dialects may be found; some geographical regions, for example, are Upstate New York and Vermont, the Upper Ohio Valley, Northern West Virginia, and South Carolina-Georgia-Low Country.

regular adjective

a word used attributively to indicate some inherent quality possessed by a person or thing.

regular determiner

in transformational grammar, one of any of three kinds of words: articles, demonstratives, and genitives: regular determiners are mutually exclusive, that is, no more than one can precede a noun; common examples are *the, any, that, those, my, your, their.*

replacement

a morphological process (q.v.) of English in which one morpheme is semantically related to another although there is no actual phonemic connection, as *went* is the past tense of *go*; in transformational grammar, it is the transformational rule symbolized as a → b, as in the derivation of *Mary went home* from *Mary goes home.*

replacive morpheme

a segmental or suprasegmental morpheme which undergoes change when the form in which it occurs changes, as when a verb is derived from a noun, such as *bath, bather* / θ → ð / or a verb is derived from an adjective, as *safe, save* / f → v /.

residue

the same as formative (q.v.).

resonants

sounds which are produced under the influence of the pharyngeal cavity and/or the oral cavity, but involving no other voice mechanism between the vocal cords and the outside air, as [y], [w], [r], [h].

response-sentence

in structural grammar, the first utterance in a conversation except the opening one unless there is a stereotyped greeting; these sentences continue a conversation and are therefore responses to previous utterances of another speaker.

resultative phrase

in structural grammar, a phrase formed by the combination of the auxiliary *be* and the past participle of the verb, as *he is finished, they are gone.*

retroflex stop

the result when, in articulation, the apex of the tongue touches the roof of the mouth back of the alveolar ridge; also called domal or calcuminal stop.

rhetorician

a scholar concerned with rhetoric, or the art of speaking and writing effectively.

root (also called base)

the term indicates the morpheme (q.v.) in a combination of two or more morphemes, which carries the principal part of the meaning of the whole, as *green*-ness or *nois-i*-ly.

root creation

the invention of an entirely new word, often through the imitation of some sound, such as *ping-pong* or *flabbergast.*

rounded sound

any sound produced with the lips partly open and to some degree pursed and protruded.

S

schwa

the unstressed central vowel / ə / in English, often heard in the first syllable of words such as *await, agog, arrive*; in the medial position, as in *enemy*; or in the final syllable, as in *sofa*.

secondary response

a term applied to utterances about language, especially those made with respect to some systematic study of language; expressed viewpoints on some aspect of language.

segment

the fraction of an utterance between any two immediately successive change-points of which both may be in the articulation of the same organ or may be change-points in the articulation of two different organs.

segmental phoneme

in the matter-form relationship which in linguistics is called a union of texture and structure, it is a minimum unit of distinctive sound (texture) or a specific sound (structure) which always becomes a textural constituent of the larger structure, the morpheme, the minimal unit of meaning; the segmental phonemes include the thirty-three vowel and consonant sounds in English.

selection

a special kind of agreement or concord found in cases where correlated suffixes make it impossible to substitute a form without a suffix for one with it.

semanteme

that unit of a word with which an inflectional morpheme

combines in the word to form a syntagm (q.v.).

semantic categories

the term indicates the specific directions in which words change in meaning as noted from linguistic history, including specialization, extension, radiation, metaphor, concretization, and deterioration (q.v.).

semantic change

the same as semantic shift (q.v.).

semantic markers

terms or signs which indicate the categories of meanings applicable to the lexical items of a sentence, somewhat similar to the classifications of meanings used in dictionaries.

semantics

the study of the meanings of speech forms, particularly of the evolutionary development and change of words or word-groups; in logic, the term refers to the relation between signs or symbols and what they signify.

semantic shift

a phenomenon in the historical evolution of a language whereby a word undergoes a change (or changes) in meaning, application, or value; for examples, see specialization, radiation, metaphor, concretization.

semantic variables

linguistic factors capable of variation or change which can have an influence upon meaning; the more common variables are: intonation, stress, pause (juncture), prolongation, and pacing.

sememe

the meaning or semantic content which may be taken from a morpheme; this appears, however, to be meaning in the sense of differential meaning only; from another point of view, in a given ideolect, a morpheme is said to have a sememe, a constant and unique meaning, a feature of the real world that is pointed to or signaled about by one or more of its phonemes.

semiology

the science of, or scientific study of, signs and/or sign language.

semiotician

in general, a student of the science of signs; in linguistics, a student of signs and symbols as modes of communication.

semiotic theory

any ordered process devised to produce a systematic explanation of the meaning of signs, or the relation of signs as stimuli to the responses they elicit.

semi-sentence

a string of language units which are in some way grammatically ill-formed, such as "Include me out," or "I have underconfidence in you." Such utterances as these which can be understood, are called semi-sentences, the set SS, while some which are not readily understood, such as "The dog sinceres the boy," are referred to as the set NS of nonsense strings.

semivowel

vowel-like sounds found in consonantal positions in that they are always in the same syllable with a true vowel;

in English the semivowels are / j w /; the glide / h / consistently acts like a semivowel, the liquids / l r / sometimes so act. See Appendix D.

semology

the study of meaning as an aspect of language.

semons

symbols devised to indicate the basic semantic components, usually with reference to a definite set of relationships, such as those used in mapping kinsmen, wherein ♂ stands for *male*, ♀ for *female*, G¹ for the first ascending generation (father, mother, aunts, uncles), *etc.*

sentence

in structural grammar, as much of the uninterrupted utterance of one speaker as is included between the beginning of the utterance and the pause which ends a sentence-final contour (q.v.), or between two such pauses.

sentence-final contour

in structural grammar, any one of several combinations of pitch and juncture which indicate the end of the sentence; the two most common, by way of example, are the level pitch /2/ followed by the rising double-bar juncture / || /, or the drop in pitch from /3/ to /1/ followed by a double cross juncture / # /.

sentence-modifier

in structural grammar, a structure of modification (q.v.) whose head is a structure of predication (q.v.) containing a finite verb.

sentence negation

that type of structure which permits (a) the occurrence

of the *either-clause,* or (b) the negative appositive tag, or (c) the question tag without *not,* to note only the more common instances; these are illustrated by: (a) "They were quite late, but we were not early, either." (b) "Directors do not fear anyone, not even stars." (c) "Directors do not listen to suggestions, do they?" Sentence negation is also achieved by the use of various special negatives, such as *not much, not many; nothing, none; little, nowhere; scarcely anybody, hardly any.*

separable verb

one of a group of English verbs with the peculiar characteristic of consisting of two parts, appearing either together or separated by one or more other elements of a structure; the first part is a form that may stand as an independent verb, while the second may be an adverbial form or a prepositional function word, as in *take over, throw out, give up.*

sequence

an uninterrupted succession of two or more segments (q.v.).

sequence-sentence

in structural grammar, any sentence which immediately follows a situation-sentence (q.v.), a response-sentence (q.v.) or another sequence-sentence, without a change in speaker, and thus is a continuation of an utterance by the same speaker.

sequence signal

any one of several devices that link sequence-sentences (q.v.) to the sentences which precede them; these include substitutes, such as pronouns; determiners (q.v.); function nouns (q.v.); function verbs (q.v.); coordinators (q.v.); and sequence-modifiers (q.v.).

sequential sentence

a sentence which of necessity follows another sentence because it depends upon that other sentence for certain elements (a kind of word-sharing), as in *Some guests will arrive early. Others won't.* The period after *early*, which is a double cross juncture, may be replaced by a conjunction.

sequential string

in transformational grammar, the series of symbolic representations stated in the derivation which is the process of producing a sentence; also applied to an individual item or line of the series.

set theory

the theory, borrowed by linguists in large part from logic and mathematics, based on the fundamental notion of class (set) membership. See Symbols.

sex antonymy

a relationship of opposites in pairs of words, one of which bears the semantic marker *Male*, the other the semantic marker *Female*, such as *aunt* and *uncle, bride* and *groom, cow* and *bull.*

shift sign

a diacritical mark used with a phonetic symbol to indicate articulation farther front [ʌ] or farther back [.] than the normal one signified by that symbol.

short vowel

in English, any one of the simple and lax vowels /i ɨ u e o ə æ a ɔ/; the term is also used to refer to any vowel which is shortened by clipping it off in articulation.

114

sibilant

the same as blade spirant (q.v.).

significant sequence

an ordered series of consecutive linguistic elements (phonemes, for example) which carry meaning in some sense
of that word.

single bar juncture

a sound transition, marking a boundary between sounds
where there occurs a minor break or pause but with sus-
tained pitch to the point of juncture, as illustrated by any
simple sentence where there tends to be a "natural" slight
pause in the utterance following the normal structure; no
punctuation is called for. See Symbols.

situation sentence

in structural grammar, the utterance unit which begins
a conversation; these may be classified as greetings (*Hello,
Mary*), calls which may be actual names or titles or short
structures (*the girl in the red dress*), exclamations, questions, or statements which elicit a response.

skewing

the presence of an irregularity in language which is itself
characterized by predominantly regular structure, thus
producing some asymmetry; skewing is most frequently
detected in the ideolect of an individual whose speech contains a sound not found in the usual pattern.

sonorant

a sound produced when an articulator moves in such a
way that it neither stops the air flow nor constricts it in
any way that produces noise.

sound-change

a gradual change in a phoneme which results in the loss of the older form of the morpheme; this implies that meaning is not involved.

sound law

a statement of observed correspondence in sounds among a group of kindred languages, that is, a statement of the expected or regular reflexes of a protophoneme (q.v.).

sound oppositions

the phonemic contrasts that constitute the distinctive acoustive features of a language; in English, these sound oppositions are vocality / consonantality; tension / laxness; interruption / continuance; gravity / acuteness; compactness / diffuseness; nasality / orality; stridency / mellowness.

sound symbolism

in the opinion of some linguists, a correspondence between sound and sense or meaning, such as the phonetic intensives (q.v.); the term could be applied to the symbols used to represent the phonetic alphabet, but this is not its usual usage.

specialization

a category of semantic change which narrows the meaning of a word which had earlier applied to a group of objects or ideas resembling each other to one object or idea from the group; for example, the word *deer* once meant "any wild quadruped" but came to have the specific meaning of the present.

speech community

any group of people who are in fairly close and continuous

communication with each other; such communities may be local or areal, but may override geographic limits as do groups such as an occupational community, represented by the medical profession, or a social community, such as "club women." The consistent, distinctive language practices of such a community may be thought of as a kind of "dialect."

spirant

the same as fricative (q.v.).

sporadic sound shift

occasional phonetic changes stimulated in a situation where, for example, a sound disappears in one part of an area but survives in another part of the same general area, with a mixed condition in the portion between; this type of shift tends to obscure word origins.

standard language

from a linguistic point of view, a language spoken by a group or by groups of people, whose dialects have become sufficiently uniform so that there is no loss of or interference with communication.

standing sentence

a statement of fact or believed fact made in the absence of the fact which can, nevertheless, elicit agreement or disagreement on the basis of collateral information, as "There is a bridge across this river two miles downstream."

stem

that form of an inflectible word which is taken as the norm from which the other members in the paradigm are formed.

step format

a schematic arrangement of structural units on separate lines so that the eye will step down from one unit to the next, as from subject structure to verb structure to complement; the format is also useful in indicating the direction of modification within and between structural elements.

stimulus meaning

the meaning of an utterance, as understood, rightly or wrongly, by a hearer, which causes in the hearer a reaction of assent or dissent.

stop

the resulting sound (actually absence of sound), when an articulator (q.v.) causes a momentary but complete interruption of the air stream with a voiceless consonant / p t k c / or with a voiced obstruent / b d g j /; also called a plosive.

stress

the degree of loudness with which a phoneme is uttered; most linguists recognize four such degrees, called primary, secondary, tertiary, and weak; also called loud, reduced loud, medial, and weak; see Symbols; to put it another way, stress is a suprasegmental phoneme (q.v.) of intonational volume, indicating the relative loudness of an utterance.

stress modification

a morphological process of English in which grammatical function is indicated by some exchange in the stress pattern, as *cómpact* (noun) and *compáct* (adjective) or *ínvalid* (noun) and *inválid* (adjective).

stridency

a distinctive acoustic feature of English characterized by the sharpness of articulation in the fricatives / s š z ž /.

strings

in generative grammar, the grammatical representations of sentences, in which each sentence may have more than one representation; for example, the two strings below are both representations of the same sentence, *The dog barked,*
    (a) Noun Phrase + Complete Predicate
    (b) Article + Noun + Complete Predicate

structural comparability

in historical linguistics, a quality found in languages of the same family, that is, derived from a common linguistic ancestor.

structural grammar

a systematized method for the study of language founded upon the concept of structure as a basis for the description and analysis of the development and status of its linguistic elements.

structural grammarian

that type of linguist who seeks to describe English not as some people think it should be, but as it is, and to develop methods of describing language that are free from subjective judgments.

structural meaning

a meaning, not lexical, of any structure, or part thereof, whether sentence, clause, or phrase, as derived from position and relationship to other structures or parts thereof; often illustrated by means of a "non-sense" passage, such as, *"The cardigs fralled the tortig shump."* From position and inflectional endings, it may be deduced that *cardigs* is a plural subject, that *fralled* is a verb in the past tense, and that *tortig* is an adjective modifying the singular object *shump*.

structure

in general, the form of an utterance, whether it be based on phonemic, morphemic, or syntactic considerations.

strucrure of complementation

that one of the four basic types of syntactic structures which consists of two components: a verbal element and a complement, as in *tell the truth*.

structure of coordination

one of the four basic types of syntactic structures in which equal grammatical units (the same parts of speech) appear, usually joined by a connective function word, such as *needles* and *pins* or *rain* or *shine*.

structure of modification

one of the four basic types of syntactic structures; this one is composed of a head (q.v.) and a modifier (q.v.) as in *poor people* or *notably inferior*.

structure of predication

that one of the four basic types of syntactic structures which is composed of a nominal element (subject) and a predicate, as in *rain continued falling* or *honesty pays*.

structure word

in transformational grammar, one of a class of words, including auxiliary verbs, prepositions, and conjunctions, which convey no lexical meaning standing alone, but serve to give order and meaningful sequence to form words (q.v.).

sub-morphemic differentials

rhyme sounds and assonances which occur in unrelated environments but which intersect others that are related and meaningful.

substitute group

a group of words which may be replaced as a group by one same substitute, as when a verb is substituted for an entire clause.

substitute word

the term refers to a word, lacking a lexical meaning, which systematically substitutes for a full word (q.v.); in English, the substitute words include all personal, possessive, and relative pronouns, the expletives, and the deictic (q.v.) adverbs of time and place.

suffix

an affix which always appears with a base to which it is bound and which it follows, such as {-ment}, {-ness}, {-ate}, {-ful}, {-ize}, etc.

superfixes

stress phonemes which appear to be superimposed on the segmental phonemes and which help to determine the function of morphemes, especially when two forms are identical in their segmental phonemes, as in the examples given under stress modification (q.v.).

superlative morpheme

the morpheme {-est}, which, added to an adjective, produces the superlative degree, as short, shortest.

suppletion

the term refers to those instances in which the comparative and superlative forms of an adjective are dissimilar from the plain form rather than formed by adding {*-er*} and {*-est*} to the plain form; the term also applies to other classes in addition to adjectives, such as pronouns, and some verbs and adverbs.

suppletive alternates

in the case of words which have functional forms which have different stems from the plain forms, the different forms within a paradigm are alternants, such as *we ~ us, they ~ them, who ~ whom, etc.*

suppletive form

a form whose components are irregular, such as what is known, in traditional grammar, as an irregular past tense, as *went,* or an irregular comparative, as *worse;* note that all components, stem and accompanying elements, must be irregular; to put it another way, any paradigmatic form having a different stem from the plain form in instances referred to as suppletion (q.v.).

suprasegmental phonemes

a set of phonemes consisting of stresses, pitches, and junctures; they appear to some linguists to be like an extra layer of structure above the basic segmental phonemes (q.v.); something of the force of stress and pitch may be seen from such an example as *Whére àre yòu góing?* as distinct from *Whère àre yóu gòing?*

suprasegmental transcription

the written manner of indicating a suprasegmental phoneme. See Symbols for stress, pitch, juncture.

surface structure

the term has reference to the fact that two statements may appear superficially to be quite similar, yet many linguists believe that there is, in addition, a deep structure (q.v.) which would show the statements to be quite different.

syllabary

a writing system in which individual symbols represent syllables rather than letters; English, though based on an alphabet, uses some such symbols, as $ or & or +.

syllabic

a phoneme which constitutes the peak (q.v.) of a phonemic syllable.

syllabic morpheme

the term is applied to a bound morpheme, usually functioning as a prefix, suffix, or inflectional ending; however, such a morpheme may sometimes act as a base, as {-duce} in reduce.

synchronic

the term refers to the study of language or a linguistic feature as it stands at a certain time or stage in its development; not to be confused with diachronic (q.v.).

synchronic description

the formulation of descriptive statements about a language as it stands at a given time without regard to its historical evolution or its relationship to other languages.

synchronic linguistics

that branch of the study of language which seeks to identify and describe the sounds of a current language and the system of sounds which they constitute.

syncretion

the process whereby the pronoun forms *you* and *it* remain unchanged whether used as subject or complement without use of a suffix, and hence do not fit into the paradigm of the pronouns.

syncretize

to fuse two or more inflectional forms that were originally different, as in declensional cases or conjugational endings, such as the past tense and past participle of many verbs, which are now the same in the inflectional ending {-ed}.

synonymity

the sameness or close similarity in meaning of two words in a language; this notion is rejected by some linguists who claim that no two linguistic forms are ever synonymous.

syntactic ambiguity

an arrangement of words which is not in accord with any of the syntactic patterns of English. A commonplace example is in the occurrence of an adjective followed by a possessive noun followed by another noun, as in *plain woman's hat*, raising the problem of ambiguity in whether the adjective *plain* applies to the *woman* or to the *hat*.

syntactic analysis

the analysis of language structures with regard to word order, word groups, and their relationships to each other and to preceding or following structures.

syntactic patterns

patterns of word order and position, based upon syntax, which are inherent in the language, as when three adjectives precede a noun, there is a specific order in which the adjectives must occur; another familiar example is the traditional "squinting" or "cross-eyed" modifier.

syntagm

a unit of meaning, yet not a word, composed of an inflectional ending combined with a semanteme (q.v.).

syntagma

a syntactic group of morphemes comprising a compound word taken as a unit of two words, the unit not identical with the combined forms or meanings of its elements, such as *black market, paper clip, executive secretary;* there are, however, differences of opinion over this term which have not been resolved.

syntagmatic relations

the relationship of words and word-groups to other words and word-groups according to their structural functions.

syntagmeme

a word-group, such as *the small brown dog;* comparable to the "phrase" of traditional grammar.

syntax

the relationship of words to one another, as when we note that plural subjects are accompanied by plural verbs; also the arrangement and relationship of words in word-groups, phrases, clauses, and sentences; also the branch of linguistics which studies these phases of language.

systematics

more properly, systematic linguistics, the study of language data in relation to systems, that is, systems of relationships in a current language, with historical aspects considered irrelevant.

tactical rules

the rules for combining the phonemes of a language, of which every language has its own set. See phonological construction.

tagma

a tentatively identified tagmeme (q.v.) which is perceived by tracing formal and semantic resemblances from string (q.v.) to string in a corpus (q.v.).

tagmeme

a composite view of the basic composite taxemes (q.v.) of a linguistic form at any one specific layer of structure (q.v.), such as the total arrangement features of the form *regularity* considered as an entity; to put it another way, a minimum functional segment of a sentence type in which the sentence type is divided according to grammatical functional parts rather than phonological or lexical parts; the tagmeme was formerly called grammeme.

taxeme

a simple, complex, or composite feature of grammatical arrangement of which there are four types: order (word or morpheme order); modulation (phonemes of stress or pitch); phonetic modification (such as in *reg*al to *reg*ular); and selection (choice of verb, adjective, *etc.*).

taxonomic linguistics

that branch of language study which is concerned with discovering and recording classes or classifications of various aspects of a language or of languages, including the phonetics.

telescoping

a process in which parts of two distinct words are combined to form a new word, either a serious blend (q.v.) or a humorous portmanteau (q.v.).

tense morpheme

also called agreement morpheme, it is that morpheme which indicates the present or past tense of a verb. See Symbols Tn, Pres, Pas.

tense phoneme

a phoneme uttered with the tongue and jaw relatively tense, as in the voiceless consonants /pfθtšchk/.

tension

an acoustic feature of English, characterized by a relative tenseness of tongue and jaw in the act of articulation, as in the voiceless consonants and the complex vowels.

terminal contour

the intonation pattern that accompanies the obligatory close juncture /#/; more simply, the sound pattern usually heard at the end of a sentence; English has two terminal contours: high rising /3/ which produces an abrupt voice cut-off, and high falling /3/ — /1/ which produces a gradual voice-fade.

terminal junctures

pauses of varying lengths, some very short, following various methods of cutting off speech, such as single-bar, double-bar, and double-cross junctures (q.v.).

terminal string

in transformational grammar, the final line in the series

128

of lines that constitute a derivation (q.v.).

tertiary response

the term refers to utterances on the subject of language, in this case the speaker's customary reaction when doubt is cast upon his secondary response (q.v.); according to Leonard Bloomfield, the tertiary response is characterized by indignation, anger, hostility.

textural intensity

the use of the sound element in language for aesthetic purposes, controlling it for special effects upon the form, meaning, and value of linguistic units; the soliloquys of Shakespeare, the poetry of Edgar Allan Poe and Gerard Manley Hopkins, and the prose of D. H. Lawrence and Ernest Hemingway abound with illustrations.

texture

the specific phonemic constituents of a linguistic form or structure, as /h/, /aw/, and /s/ are the phonemic texture of the word *house* /haws/.

tonality

the level of a voiced speech sound with particular reference to pitch.

toneme

a suggested substitute for the term suprasegmental phoneme (q.v.); some linguists do not approve of this suggestion.

transfer

the process by which a wholly new meaning becomes attached to a word as a result of some similarity, association, or other relationship of the new meaning to one of the old meanings, as in the case of *buxom* or *wench*.

transformation

the process of deriving, at least in theory, all other sentences of a language from a core of kernel sentences (q.v.).

transformational analyst

a linguist who bases his analysis of language upon the application of the rules of transformation (q.v.).

transformational grammar

also called immediate-constituent grammar, generative grammar, or generative transformational grammar, it is characterized chiefly by the tenet that word classes can be identified only by their distribution and the formal characteristics that they share; it views sentences as being made up of two-part constructions on a series of levels, beginning with a kernel sentence (q.v.).

transformed sentence

a sentence which has been produced by derivation, using a transformation rule, from the binary constituents of a kernel sentence (q.v.).

transforms

(used as a noun) the rules for making grammatical transformations (q.v.); (used as a verb, singular) the technique of applying these rules.

transitive construction

the term is applied to a group of two-word verb constructions with a stress pattern /ˆˊ/ or /ˊˆ/; such constructions (also including one-word verbs) when followed by a nominal, traditionally called the direct object, may, in turn, be followed by an adverb; some such verbs, but not all, may be followed by a direct object and an objective complement; still another group may be followed by both a direct and an indirect object (q.v.).

transliteration

the process of representing the phonemes in the "alphabet" of one language by phonemes in another language, as the Greek Σ (sigma) is represented by the Roman S.

trill

a sound which is produced when the tip of the tongue is set momentarily in vibration.

U

ultimate constituents

the minimal elements reached when immediate constituents are divided and subdivided as far as possible.

uninflectible

the term applied to those classes of words which do not undergo changes of form by adding the suffixes which are the inflectional endings; in English, the term applies to all classes of words except nouns, verbs, and pronouns.

unvoiced

also termed voiceless, it is a sound uttered without any hum of vibration of the vocal cords, a feature of all tense consonants in English.

upturn

a term designating a rise in pitch, most noticeable as the terminal rise on the last syllable of an interrogative construction; it is accompanied by a double-bar juncture /|||/ which corresponds on a fairly high level to a question mark.

uvular sound

a flap (q.v.) made by touching the back of the tongue to the back of the velum or to the uvula, as in [R] or the nasal [ŋ].

V

valence

the term refers to the privileges and limitations of occurrence of a linguistic unit in respect to other linguistic units with which it is used; this is in contrast to its use for its meaning in a communication.

velar sound

a sound produced with the back of the tongue touching or nearing the soft palate, as /k/ or /g/; the phonemes /ŋ/ and /w/ are regularly velar.

verbal nexus

the term refers to a compound word in which a verb form is the linking element which may be said to hold the word together, as in house*keep*ing and sight*see*ing.

verbal phrase

in structural grammar, the second of the two constituents in the simplest form of English sentence; this phrase is known in traditional grammar as the predicate.

verbal taboos

words whose use is frowned upon in various social circles for various reasons, usually connected with notions of politeness, taste, the avoidance of vulgarity or of giving offense to members of a race, nationality, color, or religion, *etc*.

verbform

the form of a word which may belong to more than one form class (q.v.), when it is functioning as a verb, even though its spelling and sound may be identical when it is functioning in another form class, as *trip* (verb, to stumble) and *trip* (noun, a journey).

verb phrase

in generative grammar, the second of the two structural units of which a kernel sentence is composed, as in S→ NP + VP; a verb phrase usually consists of an auxiliary, a main verb, and an optional noun phrase similar to the traditional complement; in structural grammar, the term refers to a structure composed of a main verb with its auxiliaries, if any, which functions as the core of a verbal phrase (q.v.).

verb-substitute

the verb *do*, the only true verb-substitute in English, which may substitute for any verb form, including that of full verb.

vocalic

the term refers to the syllable-forming capacity of the vowels.

vocalic inventory

the number and kind of vowel phonemes in a given ideolect (q.v.).

vocality

a distinctive acoustic feature of English, characterized by the capacity of the vowels to form syllables; the glides / y w h /, the liquids / l r /, and the nasals / m n / occasionally share this ability.

vocoids

the allophones of phonemes (vowels) which are central oral resonants, produced without narrowing the central mouth passage sufficiently to cause local friction noise.

voiced

a sound articulated with a resonant hum from the vibration of the local cords, a feature of all English vowels and lax consonants.

voiced phone

a speech sound produced while the vocal bands are sufficiently close together so that the air passing through the opening (glottis) between them causes them to vibrate and produce a tone.

voiceless phone

a speech sound produced while the opening (glottis) between the vocal bands is fully open so that there is free passage of air, as illustrated by any word when it is whispered.

vowel color

See color.

W

word-sharing

an instance of two joined structures in which the first is a complete sentence, but the second shares some words present in the first, as *I will go with you if I may (go with you)* or *He will come home soon if he can (come home soon).*

word-stock

the lexicon of a given language, that is, the sum total of all its lexical units: words, compound words, and idioms.

Z

zero allomorph

the "fictitious" form of an allomorph of an affix used to fit a form which lacks the affix into the pattern of a paradigm, as the word *sheep* or *deer* may be said to have a zero allomorph of the plural morpheme, since they are plurals which lack the /-s/, /-es/, or /-en/ ending. See zero element.

zero element

the absence of sound which results from the absence of an addition to or modification of a word and which implies meaning, as singular *chair* may be said to have zero suffix as compared to the plural *chair-s;* also applied to the loss of a minimum stressed syllable in a dialect pronunciation, as in *secret'ry* (making it a three-syllable word).

zero stress

a term applied to the weakest stress which is often left unmarked but may be indicated by [ᵁ].

Appendix A
Abbreviations and Symbols

Adv	Adverb
Af	Affix
Aux	Auxiliary verb
Comp	Subjective complement
Dem	Demonstrative
Loc	Adverb of location
Man	Adverb of manner
Mv	Main verb
N	Uninflected noun
Nom	Nominal
N_{am}	Animate noun
N_c	Count noun
N_{mass}	Mass noun
N_{pr}	Proper noun
N_{masc}	Masculine noun
N_{in}	Inanimate noun
N_{ab}	Abstract noun
N_{com}	Common noun
N_{fem}	Feminine noun
N_{neu}	Neuter noun
N_{quan}	Noun of quantity
Pred	Predicate complement
S	Sentence
Tm	Adverb of time
V	Verb
NP	Noun phrase
NP_s	Noun phrase as subject
NP_p	Noun phrase as predictate
VP	Verb phrase
V_i	Intransitive verb
V_t	Transitive verb
V_c	Copulative verb
T	Article

Appendix A (continued)

→	Stands for "may be written"
⟹	Indicates a transformation
∞	Indicates a morphological alternation
{ }	Indicates a morphemic representation or a morpheme under analysis
~	Indicates a phonological alternation
∅	Called a null; indicates an open position
/ /	Enclose a phonemic transcription
(′)	the suprasegmental phoneme of maximum stress
(^)	phoneme of major stress
(`)	phoneme of minor stress
(˘)	phoneme of minimum stress
(+)	open juncture, setting morphemic boundaries
(/)	optional internal close juncture, setting word group boundaries
(//)	obligatory internal close juncture, setting phrasal and clausal boundaries
(#)	obligatory terminal close juncture, setting sentence boundaries
>	indicates "developed to" or "became."
<	indicates "developed from."
—	indicates "corresponds to."
*	signifies a non-permitted structure.
[ ]	encloses phonetic symbols.
< >	encloses grapheme symbols.
(4)	highest intonation (pitch) level.
(3)	high intonation level.
(2)	normal intonation level.
(1)	low intonation level.
↗	indicates rising inflection.
↘	indicates falling inflection.
-	(hyphen) indicates simple concatenation, W-X-Y-Z.

Appendix A (continued)

Used Chiefly in Transformational Grammar.

Det .... Determiner.
Predet ..... Predeterminer.
Postdet .... Postdeterminer.
Gen .... Genitive.
Pro$_d$ .... a "pro" determiner.
Pro$_n$ .... a "pro" form of noun.
Tn .... tense morpheme.

Symbols for Generalized Morphemes.

{Z$_1$} .... Agreement morpheme.
{Z$_2$} .... Plural morpheme.
{Z$_3$} .... Genitive morpheme.
{-en} ...... Past participle morpheme.
{-ing} ..... Present participle morpheme.
{Pres} ..... Present tense morpheme.
{Pas} ...... Past tense morpheme.
{D$_1$} ...... Past tense of verbs which add -ed.
{D$_2$} ...... Past tense of verbs which change root vowel.
{Q} .... Interrogative morpheme.
{NG} ...... Negative morpheme.
{Imp} ..... Imperative morpheme.
{Emph} ... Emphatic morpheme.

Some Common Symbols Used in Set Theory.

$\in$ signifies "is a member of."
$\notin$ signifies "is not a member of."
$\subseteq$ means "are equal in relation to a given member."
$\subset$ means "is a proper part or sub-set of."
$\cup$ indicates union of two sets.
$\cap$ indicates intersection or membership in two sets.
$\vee$ indicates logical disjunction.
$\equiv$ signifies "if and only if."
$\supset$ signifies "if . . . then."
$+$ indicates "or" in the exclusive sense.
{ }   enclose a set.
( )   enclose an ordered set.

Appendix B

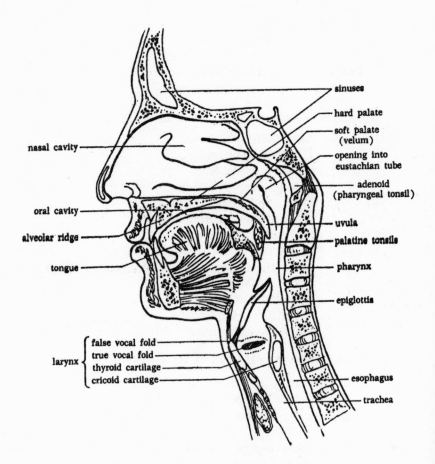

Fig. 1 The physical organs of speech.

Appendix B

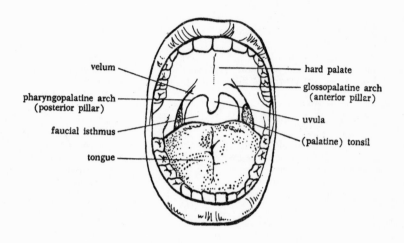

Fig. 2 Front view of the oral cavity.

Illustrations taken from Ralph R. Leutenegger, *The Sounds of American English*, Chicago, Scott, Foresman and Co., 1963, and used by permission.

Appendix C
PHONEMIC ALPHABET
(Simplified version, applicable to American English)

Vowel sounds		Consonant sounds	
Symbol	Key words	Symbol	Key words
[i]	see, eat, key	[p]	part, rope, stopped
[I]	sit, here, women, hymn	[b]	be, rubbed, dab
[e]	ache, aim, great, grey	[t]	to, debt, might, indict
[ɛ]	end, says, friend, any	[d]	do, add, could, ode
[æ]	can't, half, laugh	[k]	keep, sick, ache, walk
[ɜ]	earn, worse, germ, journey	[g]	give, egg, guest
[ɚ]	ladder, liar, sailor	[f]	fame, off, phrase, laugh
[ʌ]	up, tough, does, gull	[v]	vest, of, have
[ə]	sofa, famous, kingdom, bargain	[θ]	thin, think, through
[u]	food, rude, through, blue	[ƌ]	the, these
[U]	book, wolf, could	[s]	seem, miss, scent
[o]	hope, though, goes, shoulder	[z]	zoo, fuzz, raise
[ɔ]	all, cough, raw, gone	[ʃ] or [š]	ship, sugar, issue
[a]	farm, hat, honest	[ʒ] or [ž]	leisure, treasure
[aI]	sky, write, aisle, lye, pie	[h]	he, hat, whole
[au]	out, hour, bough, crowd	[m]	milk, money, comb
[ɔI]	boy, broil, boil	[m̩]	chasm, rhythm
		[n]	no, inn, pneumonia
		[n̩]	sadden, botany
		[l]	lake, let, tell
		[l̩]	saddle, rattle
		[w]	wig, language, wake
		[hw]	whig, whisper
		[r]	red, radish, wrist
		[j]	yes, onion, yank
		[tʃ] or [č]	chew, feature, cello
		[dʒ] or [j]	just, rage, dodge
		[ŋ]	sing, tongue, anchor

144

Consonant Chart
(Applicable to American English)

	Bilabial	Labio-dental	Apico-dental	Apico-alveolar	Fronto-palatal	Dorso-velar	Uvular	Glottal
Stops	p b			t d	(c f)	k g		ʔ
Fricatives	(φ β)	f v	θ d̆	(ʃ̥ ʃ)		(x ɣ)		h ɦ
Sibilants				s z	š ž			
Affricates				č ǰ				
Flaps & Trills				r̊ (r̈)			(R̈)	
Nasals	m	(ɱ)	(n̥) n	(ɲ)				
Laterals				l̥ l ɫ	(ʎ)	ɫ L		
Semi-vowels	w̥ w (ʙ̇)			r̥ r	j	w̥ w (ʙ̇)		

Diacritics: Syllabic [ˌ]; Voiceless [˳]: Aspirated [ᶜ];
Fortis [⊓]; Lenis [⊔]; Voiced [ᵥ];
Rounded [⌣]; Unrounded [∞].
Shift signs: Forward [ʌ]; Backward [●].

The Vowel Quadrangle (applicable to American English)

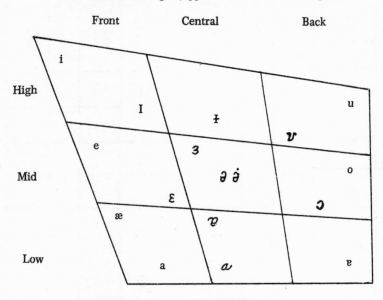

Vowel Shift Signs

Half-long [.]; Long [:]; Over-long [::];
Short [ᴜ];
Raised [⊥]; Lowered [ᴛ]; Fronted [◂];
Retracted [▸];
Rounded [ᴜ]; Unrounded [ᴍ]; Nasalized [~];
Voiceless [ₒ]; Non-syllabic [ᴖ]; Strongest stress [ʺ];
Strong stress [']; Medium stress [₊].

Phonemes

Stops: / p t k b d g /
Affricates: / c j /
Fricatives: / f v /
Sibilants: / s š z ž /
Nasals: / m n /
Lateral: / l /
Semi-vowels: / r w y h /

Vowels:

	Front	Cen	Back
High	i	ɨ	u
Mid	e	ə	o
Low	æ	a	ɔ

Stresses: / ˊ ˄ ˋ ᵁ /
Pitches: / 1 2 3 4 /
Junctures: / + / // # /

ALSO BY TIMOTHY W. RYBACK

The Last Survivor: Legacies of Dachau

Hitler's Private Library

Adolf Hitler, thirty-six, posing with his books
in his first Munich apartment.

Hitler's
Private Library

THE BOOKS THAT SHAPED HIS LIFE

Timothy W. Ryback

ALFRED A. KNOPF   NEW YORK   2008

THIS IS A BORZOI BOOK
PUBLISHED BY ALFRED A. KNOPF

Copyright © 2008 by Timothy W. Ryback

All rights reserved. Published in the United States by Alfred A. Knopf,
a division of Random House, Inc., New York, and in Canada by Random House
of Canada Limited, Toronto.

www.aaknopf.com

Knopf, Borzoi Books, and the colophon are registered trademarks
of Random House, Inc.

Grateful acknowledgment is made to Mary Sharp for permission
to reprint previously published material from *This Is the Enemy* by
Frederick C. Oechsner (Boston: Little, Brown, 1942).

Library of Congress Cataloging-in-Publication Data
Ryback, Timothy W.
Hitler's private library : the books that shaped the man / by
Timothy W. Ryback.—1st ed.
p.   cm.
Includes bibliographical references and index.
ISBN 978-1-4000-4204-3
1. Hitler, Adolf, 1889–1945—Books and reading. 2. Hitler, Adolf, 1889–1945—
Knowledge and learning. 3. Germany—History—1933–1945.
4. Library of Congress—Catalogs. I. Title.
DD247.H5R94 2008   027.1092—dc22   2008022010

Manufactured in the United States of America

First Edition